the
church of
us vs.
them

the church of us vs. them

Freedom from a Faith
That Feeds on Making Enemies

DAVID E. FITCH

BrazosPress

a division of Baker Publishing Group
Grand Rapids, Michigan

Published by Brazos Press
a division of Baker Publishing Group
PO Box 6287, Grand Rapids, MI 49516-6287
www.brazospress.com

Printed in the United States of America

Library of Congress Cataloging-in-Publication Data
Names: Fitch, David E., 1956– author.
Title: The church of us vs. them : freedom from a faith that feeds on making enemies / David E. Fitch.
Description: Grand Rapids : Brazos Press, a division of Baker Publishing Group, 2019. | Includes bibliographical references and index.
Identifiers: LCCN 2018053681 | ISBN 9781587434143 (cloth)
Subjects: LCSH: Christianity and culture. | Mission of the church. | Christianity— United States.
Classification: LCC BR115.C8 F595 2019 | DDC 261—dc23
LC record available at https://lccn.loc.gov/2018053681

In keeping with biblical principles of creation stewardship, Baker Publishing Group advocates the responsible use of our natural resources. As a member of the Green Press Initiative, our company uses recycled paper when possible. The text paper of this book is composed in part of post-consumer waste.

19 20 21 22 23 24 25   7 6 5 4 3 2 1

green press
INITIATIVE

To Rae Ann, my wife of almost twenty years—
a testament to her patience and long-suffering
in the unwinding of life's antagonisms.

contents

preface

I believe the Bible is the authoritative Word of God for the church. I have signed a doctrinal statement affirming the inerrancy of Scripture (although I made note that it was too liberal for me). I believe conversion is central to the Christian life, and I believe all Christians are called to participate in God's mission of salvation, justice, and healing to the world. These beliefs pretty much make me an evangelical in the traditional use of the term. But something has happened in our culture these past few decades with regard to evangelicals and other like-minded Christians. Evangelicals have allowed these fundamental convictions to become the source of division, anger, and antagonism among us and between us and the people around us. In the process we've become the church of us vs. them. I contend that this has been disastrous for our witness to Christ and his lordship and salvation in North America. Many people no longer want to be identified as an evangelical as a result.

So in this book I examine how this happened. I look at how evangelicals' core beliefs morphed to change us into the church of us vs. them, and then at how to move beyond this. In the book, I do not provide a careful exposition of these doctrines themselves. This book isn't a systematic theology in any sense of the term.

Instead, I am trying to show how these beliefs and the ways we practice these beliefs have shaped us evangelicals, and other Christians alongside us, as a particular kind of people: an antagonistic people. In this sense, I'm writing a kind of political theology, answering the question, How do our beliefs and practices shape us to be a particular kind of people for mission in the world? In the process, I'm pushing for a renewed practice of reading Scripture, doing evangelism, and engaging culture that renews our presence as the witnesses to the reign of Jesus Christ as Lord in our culture.

I first explored these beliefs in this manner in the book *The End of Evangelicalism?* way back in 2011.[1] This present book seeks to engage on a popular level much of what I learned back then and have worked out in daily life as a church pastor/coach/professor since then. So this book often borrows from that book. Nonetheless, *The Church of Us vs. Them* is a completely different book seeking to apply those lessons to the current day. But for those interested in more of the theology and ideological analysis that drives this book, I encourage you to read *The End of Evangelicalism?* and to read the endnotes in this book, where I have put most of the academic work that undergirds this book's claims.

The stories in this book are purposefully disguised to protect the identities of the people involved. I not only change the names of people in the stories, I sometimes change the gender and other details of the characters, and in a couple cases I amalgamate the details of two people into one story. I do this with the intent of holding the integrity of stories intact while protecting the identities of the people involved.

Many thanks go to the people who made the writing of this book possible. My colleague Scot McKnight urged me to do it. Scott Boren, who had worked with me on a previous book, sold me on the idea that this book was important and worth doing. He helped organize my notes and lectures in the early stages of writing. Thanks to both Scot(t)s. Northern Seminary provided me a sabbatical, during which some of the work on this book was done. Northern has been such a support to my work and an amazing, exciting place for the preparation of leaders this book pushes for. Many thanks to this truly special institution. The good people of Baker Publishing Group have been great all along the way in making this book possible. Thanks to Bob Hosack for shepherding this book into the good hands of Baker. A special thanks to James Korsmo for his editing work on this book. His work improved this book greatly. Lastly, special thanks goes to my family: my wife, Rae Ann, and my son, Max. They really do make so much of my own ministry of pastoring, writing, and professoring possible.

For his glory!

introduction

Beyond Enemies?

W e're living in angry times. Wherever we go, whether church, school, city hall, or Washington, DC; whatever we watch, whether cable television, Facebook, or the local theater; and however we do things, whether by email or Twitter or telephone, in person, or in a meeting—in it all, our culture is rife with conflict. Politics is full of strife, antagonisms, and vitriol. Everybody, it seems, is caught up with warding off yet another enemy. And so, many of us are just keeping our heads down, hoping to get through another day, causing as little trouble as we can. Something has gone terribly wrong in our country, and we don't know what to do about it.

Meanwhile, the church appears little different. Christians appear to be caught up in the same antagonism and disgust for one another that is evident elsewhere. We ourselves have become known for our own enemy making. We fight among ourselves on the various media while the world looks on. What has happened? Christians have failed to be known by our love, and the question is, Why?

How is it that Christians have failed at this most prescient moment to be a people of reconciliation and renewal in the face of all this tumult? And how do we get out of the mess to become a reconciling presence in the world through Jesus Christ? How can Christians respond in the face of this failure, to be the presence of his love, reconciliation, and healing in a world torn by strife and ugly conflict? And how can we keep our integrity and love for justice in the process? Imagine the amazing witness we'd have at this present time if we were known by the way we reconcile with, love, and restore one another. This book is born out of these questions. It asks, How can we be shaped by Christ into becoming these kinds of people? How can we become the reconciling presence of Christ in the world?

I Remember

I remember the summer of 1969, when as a young boy I saw the television pictures of Neil Armstrong walking on the moon. His words—"That's one small step for man, one giant leap for mankind"—are now among the most recognized phrases ever spoken. But just a few years later the Apollo 13 accident happened. Here we remember the words, paraphrased and made famous in the movie *Apollo 13*—"Houston, we have a problem"—spoken by mission commander Jim Lovell after an explosion occurred on their ship. With Armstrong, there was this incredible surge of optimism in North America; humanity, we thought, could accomplish just about anything we put our mind to. But with Apollo 13, there was a sense that something had gone terribly wrong. Within a short time, the United States had journeyed from euphoria to tragedy and was facing the reality of how little control humanity has over the mysteries of space.

Today, the church finds itself in a similar place. We remember a time not too long ago (let's call it the 1950s) when the established church occupied a powerful place in North America. This was largely a white majority North America. Protestant Christians were confident in our message, our institutions, and our authority in culture. We were oblivious to any of the negative impacts our version of Christianity was having on minority cultures. There was a sense of triumph in the air after World War II. For the "majority population" who lived in those times, Christians were part of a chosen people. We felt proud to be associated with the words "The truth is marching on."[1]

But half a century later, "we have a problem." Christians from the "majority" church are on the defensive in our culture. Our churches are divided over politics, nationalism, race, and sexuality. In many cases, Christians find ourselves resented or even rejected wholesale by our cultures. Like a spacecraft trying to get back home, we are disoriented. But unlike Apollo 13, which had a sudden explosion accompanied by flashing warning lights, this problem has crept up on us slowly. The warning lights have been so subtle that we've been able to ignore them. But not so any longer.

Supposedly, a frog sitting in water that is slowly warmed does not realize it is being cooked by the heat until it is too late, and then the frog dies. If you were simply to drop the same frog into hot water, it would jump out immediately. The problems many Christians face today in North America have crept up on us so subtly that they are now the water we swim in and we cannot recognize it. Many of us don't even see the flashing warning lights because they have become the standard by which the norm is evaluated. While the lights are going off, this creeping normalcy causes us to interpret these warnings as just another part of what it means to be a Christian today.

But deep down we know things are not as they are supposed to be. The anger, strife, and hatred that keep erupting point to the problem. And we need to name it so we can figure out how to respond. We need to look at the dashboard of this out-of-control spaceship and identify some of the lights that are flashing.

Flashing Light #1: The Loss of Christendom Influence

There was a time when many of us lived in a society that agreed
on Christianity as the right way to live. It was a majority Euro-
world's Christianity. And for those who were part of this majority,
this environment was good and comfortable. But a warning light
is flashing, telling us this world is breaking apart.

"Christendom" refers to a time period in the Middle Ages of
Western Europe when all of society (church, state, schools, work,
art) was united under the one umbrella of Christianity. Whether in
work, education, politics, family, or money, all of life was ordered
around the core beliefs in Christianity. Certainly it was never that
simple. Still, more often than not, throughout most of medieval
Europe, Christianity's influence dominated all of life.

The Reformation did little to change this Christendom frame-
work; it only divided up territories and offered various versions of
Christianity that would govern each territory—mostly Lutheran,
Reformed, or Catholic.

As Christianity moved overseas to North America, Christendom worked in ways similar to the average modern experience
of buying a car. In many American cities, competing car dealerships are built alongside one another along one big avenue. A
person in the market for a car need only make his or her way
to that general area of town and then test-drive a Ford, then
a Honda, and then a Volvo, all within a short period of time.
All the dealerships are quickly accessible on the same street. It
is assumed, in a car-driving culture, that everyone drives a car.
The only question then is, Which car best suits you? Similarly, in
North America, Christendom assumes we all live in a society that
follows Christian principles and beliefs. The question is, Which
kind of Christianity best suits you? As a result, the Christian
options in the North American version of Christendom all lined
up to compete with one another like car dealerships competing
for customers.

This backdrop of Christendom was everywhere in the North America of the 1950s. Those were the days when our parents (or grandparents) watched *The Andy Griffith Show*, with Andy attending church on Sundays and Barney singing in the choir. Billy Graham would put on a traditional evangelical Sunday service in a local football stadium and thousands showed up. Protestant churches would hold Sunday evening services and expect their regular members to bring nonpracticing Christians to hear the gospel preached. Television networks would honor Christian values in their programming. Public schools regularly allowed prayer to start the day. The government gave its nod to promote church life. Just like everybody knows you need a car to get around and work in our society, so everybody assumed you needed a church.

But the warning light is flashing to all who were once comfortable here. This Christendom world is breaking up. We cannot assume "our" Christian views will have sway like they once did. Christians naturally want to be comfortable again, but that world is gone. And so, every time sexuality or gender issues come up in our schools or local town hall meetings, or when we notice women wearing hijab at the grocery store, or when the church is criticized for its participation in racism, we, who were once the majority, want to defend that place we once called home. We divide up and go to the church "brand" that agrees with us. In the midst of these conflicts, we just want to guide the spaceship back home. But there's no going home anymore and, with every new conflict busting out in our midst, the warning lights are flashing everywhere.

Flashing Light #2: The Problem of Christendom Habits

Habits from Christendom linger on in our churches. These habits revolve around ways of relating to everyone as if they are either already Christians (like us) or should be (what's wrong with you?). Just as car manufacturers assume that everyone in North America drives a car, Christians and our churches assume a lot of things about the people and the culture around us. These Christendom habits can be broken down into three categories.

First, there are the habits based in the way we talk. Christians in Christendom assume that everyone, even those who do not belong to a church, know our language. We assume people we meet every day know what we mean when we say words like "sin," "salvation," and "repent." We assume that people we meet in everyday life know what the cross means and why designated religious holidays point to Christ. We assume that everyone, just like Billy Graham, believes what "the Bible says." As a result, we are surprised when people don't immediately understand or agree with our assertions about moral and social matters.

Second, Christians in Christendom assume people in the broader culture want to come to church; they just haven't found the right one. Because culture once agreed with us on a lot of things, such as promiscuous sexuality, excess greed, marriage, alcohol, and freedom to worship, we focused on Christian life as something that takes place primarily in a building. We expect the culture to be in sync with Christianity, even if people out there do not go to church. Many of us now sit uncomfortably in front of the TV or at the theater, not knowing what to do with a culture that defies Christian values. How can we invite anyone to church?

Last, Christians in Christendom respect spiritual leaders and expect others to do the same. Christendom trains Christians to look up to and respect clergy. Pastors are those who are educated and ordained and who hold the office of pastor by virtue of either their credentials or their effective skills at preaching and leading. In the Christendom of the fifties, it was not unusual for local governments to consult the pastors in their cities on civic matters. Christians today have the carryover habit of expecting their pastors to have authority not only in their churches but in their communities. When they are shunned or discredited, it comes as a shock.

These are the habits of Christendom that once worked so well for so many. In large parts of the US and Canada, however, churches have to work harder to attract people to services. Our language no longer connects to the people we live alongside at work or in the neighborhood. Our institutions of Christianity, and their officials, do not garner respect in our society. For those of us who had gotten used to these things, we are like fish out of water. Our reflex is to get angry when we are challenged. Our feelings get hurt when we are rejected. Our first impulse is to lash out when other Christians dare to contradict what we have believed throughout our lives. We were used to being the majority. We're used to trusting our authorities. Now we are surrounded, and we do not know how to guide this spaceship we are on that is lost in a foreign culture.

Flashing Light #3: The Christendom Tendency to Make Enemies

There's an additional flashing light that is perhaps even more ominous than the previous two: the ever-increasing tendency among Christians to make enemies with each other. Somehow, when you put the assumption that everyone is or should be a Christian together with the Christendom habits of language ("You must speak like us"), power ("Our leader is right; how dare you challenge him/her?"), and church attendance ("Why are so many people going to that church?"), defensiveness breaks out. Suddenly we find ourselves seeing other Christian churches as the competition. We no longer see other Christians as being in common life together. We instead see that church down the road—the one that doesn't "do church" the same way we do—as the enemy. And herein lies something insidious that harms our witness in this world, perhaps more than any of the other flashing lights.

For centuries the church has advanced by trying to find a new version of church that corrects or improves on the previous version.

Lutheranism arose in reaction to the corruption of Catholicism in the Middle Ages. Innocent enough. In the midst of the Reformation, Calvin promoted a different option from Luther in response to Catholicism. Fine. But then the Pietists got fed up with the "faith-alone" stodginess of mainstream Lutherans and eventually formed their own churches. The Anglican Church arose out of (King Henry's) frustration with the Roman Catholic Church; it broke away. The Wesleyan movement developed out of discontent with the moral laxity of the Anglican Church and went on to form a new church with "society meetings." The Pentecostals found speaking in tongues and did the same. And of course there is the joke that the Baptists start a new church every time there's a disagreement at the annual church business meeting.

Hundreds of years later it seems that dividing is in the DNA of Christendom. The process of forming new denominations in reaction to other denominations may have worked to foment creativity and vitality in the early years of North American Christianity.[2] But today, many years later, it seems all this dividing has taken on a new character in the midst of our changing culture. As our culture cares less about the church, we are clamoring for the loyalty of the Christians who are left. We are consolidating what power is left to have. We are defending our leaders with a new vigor, even when they fail miserably. And we seem to be surprised and increasingly upset when our culture doesn't follow our lead, or seem to be the least bit concerned about following our lead, on moral issues. Our witness, as a people, to the life, death, and resurrection of Jesus Christ has become tainted with the ugliness of enemy making. To the culture at large, the church has the look of a spaceship headed for a self-inflicted crash.

Here We Are

And so here we are, Christians, facing unparalleled challenges in our culture. Our culture is challenging us with regard to sexuality and the truth of other religions and issues of racism and the church, of justice and economics. In response, we quote the Bible. We take sides against one another. We rally people around political parties who will do our bidding. We presume people will respect our arguments and choose sides, even when people aren't interested. Because we have been so used to power, we take positions against other churches on the Bible, salvation, and even justice. We can't stop ourselves. Trying to survive, we create new modes of church and new constituencies. Christianity becomes a set of belief statements that we argue either for or against with other Christians. And the actual practice of following Jesus becomes lost in the fray.

We carry these same habits into our engagements with non-Christians. We start arguing against non-Christians whom we assume should be Christians. The bad habits of infighting now turn us against the world. In regard to economics, racism, sexuality, and other religions, we find ourselves looking for the political party that best aligns with our position. We find ourselves arming for a fight. We are indistinguishable from the world.

A recent car commercial depicts real people entering a room full of the automaker's cars. The host says that he is going to display a list of awards that this car manufacturer has won and asks them to read the awards as quickly as possible as he scrolls through them on a screen. Of course, because there are so many awards, they cannot keep up. The commercial concludes with clips of people saying they are now in the market for a car and are excited to check out this specific make of car. On the surface, this seems like a convincing commercial. Everyone is happy to discover all the new cars available. Yet the commercial works because it subtly makes each customer feel better about a prospective purchase by proving this brand of car is better than other cars. That's the way the best advertising works. It creates in us the urge to measure ourselves and our choices against the other options. Subtly we feel good because we have chosen the better option. Meanwhile, we are blind to the antagonism that is working to make us feel better about ourselves and our purchases.

This is where we are as the church in North America. We cannot help but make enemies in the way we do church in North America. As Christians, we have become blind to the antagonisms at work in our lives, both within the church and without. Old habits inherited from Christendom have shaped us to live and indeed even to thrive on antagonisms. Meanwhile, people outside the church look at us and see only conflict, anger, and even hate. Our witness to Christ is damaged. And as we enter the world, we've lost the wherewithal to engage what God is doing in Christ to save the world.

Beyond Enemies

In what follows, I aim to push us to go beyond this space of antagonism to a space I'd like to describe as "beyond enemies." This names the place I believe Christians are called to occupy in the world in and through Jesus Christ. It is a space made uniquely possible through Christ and his presence among us. It is the space that lies beyond the Christendom habits of making enemies.

The word "enemies" speaks to the way of the world that "others" the person(s) we disagree with. This is what defines an antagonism: the making of an enemy by turning someone into an "other." The world runs on antagonisms—what I call the "enemy-making machine." It's a social dynamic in which we are always forced to take sides. We then define our "selves" against someone via a position. Our identity becomes attached to this position. Our motivations and desires get aligned with this position. We start to defend ourselves at all costs. Our joys and sorrows become strangely formed around what happens day by day in the success of our position. Before we know it, we are stuck in this position, permanently ensconced in the violence of the world. In so doing, ideology comes into being, and we are thoroughly buying into it.

"Beyond" speaks to the way this place is not a middle space or a place of compromise between two positions. Rather, this space is from God, opened by the presence of Christ, and always working for something new that could not have been anticipated. If the world is ideological in the sense described above, we must get beyond the ideological. So "beyond" is not a third way that mediates between the previous two ways in conflict. It is a space where we are still able to be who we are. Indeed, we become *more* of who we are because, in this space, we can extend further into being faithful to Christ and his kingdom. And yet it escapes the current frame of anger, antagonism, and violence in the world.[3] And it is Christ's supernatural presence that breaks the hold of the antagonistic frame. He is what makes the space possible. This is the space, I contend, the church must occupy and open up in a world that is not Christian. This is the space where Christ comes to work. It is not "us vs. them"; it is the space beyond enemies.

Admittedly, such a space is hard to imagine. It seems that the church, especially since the 2016 US presidential election, has fallen deeply into the habits of positioning, anger, and coercion. The old habits of Christendom die slowly. And yet God, I contend, cannot work his mission for the world via the anger, antagonism, and violence that characterize the world apart from God. If the church is to open up a new space beyond enemies for the work of Christ in the world, it must do so by his Spirit, through his presence.

But it must happen first among ourselves. In order to enter the world, we must first become the place the world can recognize as beyond enemies. We must first deal with our own antagonisms. Once freed, we then can enter the world in peace, opening up space for Christ to work in the world. As I have argued elsewhere, this is how God has chosen to change the world through a people.[4]

The Example of Jeremy

At a recent conference, after I had finished my presentation, a man named Jeremy made a beeline from his seat to the front of the room where I was standing. He approached me quickly, told me how he had been a pastor for twelve years and how he was now ready to quit. He confessed, "It's one thing after another, conflict after conflict. I don't know how to lead anymore. They want me to give the right answers, but when I don't tell them what they want to hear, they run off down the road to another church that will. And the reality is that no one outside of the church cares. Our fights, our opinions, our squabbles over our inside church debates just don't matter. But I don't know how to lead a church out of this. I am sick of it, but it's what I was trained to do. What am I supposed to do now?"

Jeremy was seeing the flashing lights on the dashboard. Like Jim Lovell in *Apollo 13*, he was announcing, "Church, we have a problem." The church had become the church of us vs. them. And just as that rocket ship could not land on the moon, so too, we must confess with Jeremy that our way of being the church today is not landing in our culture. Our "enemy making" works against who Jesus is and what he is doing in the world.

And so, in coming to grips with the situation of the church in North America, we can ignore the flashing lights and continue in the habits we have become so comfortable in. Indeed, we can fight harder and try to build even bigger and better versions of the same churches to attract people to our buildings and programs. Or we can pause and take our churches in for a checkup on these habits we have become so used to. We can open up space for the unwinding of these antagonisms and the beginning of a new work of God among us. The old ways of Christendom will still succeed at times, maybe even enough to make us think they're working. But Christendom is waning, our churches are in survival mode, and many of our pastors are struggling. It's time to pursue a way beyond the church of us vs. them.

In what follows, we'll unwind the antagonisms that have driven the last hundred years of church in North America. We'll deconstruct the old Christendom habits that drive how we think about and practice Scripture, conversion, and even justice. We'll explore faithful ways to think about these core beliefs, ways that don't gather people by making enemies but instead gather a church into Christ's presence for his mission in the world. We'll explore how unwinding habits of the past will change our very posture and presence in our neighborhoods to meet the cultural challenges we face in mission. We'll look for ways to open up a new space beyond enemies to bring the gospel of Christ's kingdom to our culture.

1

the strife among us

Getting angry and making enemies has become such an everyday occurrence in our culture these days that many of us hardly take notice anymore. Our "Christian fighting," however, is often subtler. We judge people with a smile and some prideful condescension; meanwhile, we are simmering beneath the surface in spiteful anger. Eventually the anger does erupt and the subtlety disappears, shocking us as if it appeared from nowhere. We are left wondering what has just happened. How did things get this way?

The story of Justin illustrates what I'm talking about. He grew up as a pastor's kid in a small town in rural Indiana. He was taught everything he needed to know about God in this one rural town— what the Bible means, how to get saved, and how to be a part of a church. He learned how to read the Bible the right way, how to pray the right way, and how to have the right kind of personal relationship with Jesus. When he turned twenty-five, he moved to the big city to study at a seminary and work at a church. There he discovered that his way of doing things back home, his way of relating to God and going to church, was not the only option. He was bombarded with challenges, and this stirred up anger within. In the process, non-Christians were often dismissive of him, acting like his faith was from the Dark Ages. The main challenge for him, however, came from people who were supposed to be on the same side with him. It was inevitable that the frustration within him would start to simmer.

On top of all this, a moral failure by the pastor of his city church surfaced. The congregation wallowed in indecision as they fought over what to do next. The pastor, whom Justin had trusted, fell apart emotionally as he tried to defend himself. Divisive name-calling, slanderous rumors, and even angry shouting became commonplace—all in the name of Jesus—and it led to a church split.

Before moving to the big city, Justin thought following Jesus was clear-cut and simple. He only had to believe the Bible the way his dad had taught him and go to church, as had been done for generations. But now he entered a crisis of belief that led to an eventual emotional breakdown. He tried to be nice through it all, but beneath the surface his emotions were taking him on a roller-coaster ride. He vacillated between being angry at Christians who hurt him and vehemently defending the faith of his childhood. It took him years to make sense of it all.

I've interacted with many Justins over the years. His story illustrates the plight of many Christians in the age of Trump. The rug, it seems, has been pulled out from beneath our feet. Our beliefs crumbling, we work furiously to rebuild them. The spiritual leaders we trust fail us, and we in return lash out in pain, feeling betrayed. We react against those who question our foundation for living. When the world around us and the lives of people we love challenge the things we once learned as moral and spiritual absolutes, we are desperate to find a path but are holding a map that has lost its boundaries. At this point, we are angry at the past authority structures we once held on to. We distrust other Christians and what they are trying to do to us. This is not merely a shift in how we think about God and church. We have entered into an antagonistic mode of distrusting everything while fighting for something. As a result, we have whole generations who have left the church, who hold anger against the church, who simply find it hard to trust the church ever again. We are banging our heads against the wall of life itself as our eyes are opened to things that are just plain overwhelming. What's a person to do?

Two Common Options

When the smoke clears, most people respond in one of two ways. One group opts for the defensive posture. They dig deeper into what they already know, reentrench themselves in their "truth," and assess all other options according to the way they see things. As a result, they feel compelled to tell people what to think and how to live. This is defensive Christianity. Justin's dad encouraged him to take this route. Every time he would visit his son in the midst of crisis, he would argue more intently on why the "truth" is *the* truth. His advice for Justin was to ground himself in the established truth, move on, and just live it out boldly.

The second group opts for accommodation. Here people shift their established beliefs to assimilate in some way with the ones who challenge them. This makes for a smoother navigation than the defensive route. Justin's friends all around him could not understand why he took his faith so legalistically. Why was he so uptight, closed off, and rigid? "Be free," they told him. "Surely God wants you to be yourself and live your life to its fullest. Find the 'God' who is more generous, affirming, and gracious." Because he had heard so much about God's grace while growing up, this made some sense to him. So Justin started to accommodate. But after about five years, his life exhibited problems. He lost himself in bad sexual habits like pornography. He couldn't hold on to friends. He became devoured by the culture. His relationships with women grew shallow. He became consumed by his appetite for money. He started to crash and burn. He couldn't find his way through the worlds of post-Christendom. The way of accommodation provided him no direction through this mess.

Ironically, when Christendom (as surveyed in the introduction above) rules the way that we live and think, these two options work quite well. Defending the Christian faith can make sense to people who still look to the church with respect. They trust those in authority to tell them what to do. They can do quite well living in the cocoon. Likewise, accommodating the Christian faith to cultural values can make sense because most people in the culture are at least cultural Christians. It isn't that big of a shift to accept the broader cultural values as the basis for one's Christianity.

But for many today, Christendom no longer reigns. When people see a church defending its Christian beliefs, they grow suspicious. They are suspicious of a church that grapples to retain its diminishing power. Like a dictator grasping for what he once had, the church appears weak, coercive, and unconvincing the more it tries to defend itself.

In a similar way, when people observe a church endorsing commonly held cultural values, they shrug, thinking, "Oh, isn't that interesting?" But they don't perceive a church's decision to accommodate cultural values as having any relevance to their daily life.

Meanwhile, people inside the church see these as the only two options, and they divide against each other accordingly. People who defend traditional Christian beliefs look "across the aisle" to the people affirming cultural values. The defensive Christians accuse the accommodating Christians of falling away. On the other side, the accommodating Christians see the traditional church as behind the times, holding on to the past and becoming legalistic about it. And each side digs deeper into its position while ignoring any real engagement on the ground with real people over the things we're all trying to figure out. The fight heats up for everybody to see, which takes all our energy and leaves nothing for engaging the world with the gospel. Meanwhile, there's no reason for people outside the church to listen to Christians, because they have seen our infighting and turned away in disgust.

What's Going On?

I've had my own "Justin moments" along the way.

For instance, I grew up in a church that loved the Bible. Much of our time together in Sunday services or in youth gatherings was spent studying the Bible. Around the church, we took comfort whenever someone said that our point of view on an issue was "biblical." When it came to actual issues that we high schoolers were facing, however, like sexuality, different religious perspectives, and racism, we spent little time studying what the Bible says about these issues. The Bible, though, was something everybody in our church believed. In fact, we were taught to be wary of people who did not believe the Bible. How people viewed the Bible served as a kind of litmus test that determined who could be trusted and who could not. I found myself becoming distrustful of people outside my church who didn't believe the Bible. This included Christians who were known as "liberal." Somehow, beneath the surface, the Bible, even though we didn't use it very well on the tough issues we were facing, had become the source of antagonism in my life.

A similar thing happened around my teenage experience of Evangelism Explosion. EE, as it was called, was a popular method of evangelism back then that required us Christians to knock on the front door of a stranger. When the person answered the door, we inquired as to whether we could ask him or her some questions from a questionnaire, which inevitably led to one of the following: (a) On a scale from one to ten, if you died today, how certain are you that you would go to heaven? Or (b) Suppose that you were to die today and stand before God. If he were to say to you, "Why should I let you into my heaven?" what would you say?

What surprised me about this experience was that the strangers I encountered at their front doors were largely unconcerned about their afterlife. They were incredulous that a simple prayer to God could make a difference to their eternity. Indeed, this way of talking about salvation made no sense to them. I would walk away from several front doors asking myself how they could so casually dismiss something so singularly important to my life. Then I would think, "They don't get it; they're going to hell." Or, "These people are really lost. I feel so sorry for them." Fear and defensiveness welled up inside me, leading me to feel better about myself. After all, "I know I am in and they are out." Once again, beneath the surface (never spoken in public), a key doctrine of my church—salvation and conversion—had become a source of a troublesome antagonism in my life.

A third experience took shape in my life surrounding our church's subtle attachment to the American flag (when I lived in the US, that is). As we gathered for worship week after week, year after year, there was a pervasive sense that somehow our God was at work in our country in ways that he was not in other countries, and that we should support conservative Christian values through the government. Whether it was the Conservative party (when I lived in Canada) or the Republican party (in the US), being a good Christian got melded together with being a conservative and praying for our troops, and with supporting various military efforts. Then Jerry Falwell and the Moral Majority became prominent during the time of President Reagan. Soon I discovered myself once again being suspicious and distrustful of any Christian who voted for the other party. Though it was beneath the surface, once again a key belief about being God's people in the world had morphed into an antagonism in my life.

Through all of this, I noticed occasional outbursts of anger and defensiveness arising when Christians would engage with our schools, in town hall meetings, or with the press over issues in our city or neighborhood. We were not allowed to pray in schools or have Bible studies: "An outrage!" The schools allowed certain movies to be shown in the classroom, and the Veterans' Day parade had a Muslim cleric say a prayer for all: "How dare they!" Birth control was taught in education classes: "But the Bible says . . . " Each time an issue was discussed among us at church, or whenever a Christian or a pastor showed up at a school or city meeting, the Bible was invoked or conservative values were espoused as Christian. But it seemed to go nowhere. Years later, in today's social conflicts over sexuality, gender and racial equality, religious differences, and violence and war, it seems we are doing the same things. Just as many did back then, we Christians are becoming strangely defensive and volatile. In high school, I was shrinking from important conversations or writing people off who didn't believe like I did. The same is often the case today.

As I look back at those experiences, I've wondered what it would have been like to visit with a good therapist about these beneath-the-surface issues. Perhaps the whole church could have crowded into his or her office and gotten to the root of why some people get so angry when someone denies the accuracy of the Bible or why the topic of "conversion" makes us want to separate from people who haven't made the same decision in the same way we have. Might we be able to understand why some people go "ballistic" when the flag is moved from behind the pulpit? Just as a good marriage therapist can help a husband and wife see why each responds the way that they do, is it possible to look beneath the surface to understand what's going on that makes us feel the ways we do?

Today, amid heightened division between Christians, something deeper and more endemic seems to be going on that is defining us as Christians. It is not just the defensiveness of conservative Christians. It is equally the acerbic backlash of progressive Christians. There is equal hand-wringing on both sides whenever a Christian leader questions or applauds LGBTQ sexuality. We have seen books removed from bookstores, insults hurled. We say "Farewell so-and-so" on social media. Many churches cannot talk about the role of women in leadership for fear of being called "liberal," nor can they talk about issues involving the poor and health care for fear of being labeled "socialist." Conservatives are marginalized in progressive groups and progressives are marginalized in conservative groups. And so we are all silenced. No one wants to be the cause of dividing a church. The divisiveness of the 2016 presidential election is merely the symptom of a deeper and broader phenomenon that has come to define Christianity in North America in recent decades. We have become energized and even defined by the enemies we make and the sides we take.

What is driving us to be this way? What is causing Christians in North America to act this way?

We All Need a Little Therapy

The times are ripe for an examination of our underlying motives and perspectives. In what follows, I propose some therapy for our churches and for our lives as Christians. I go beneath the surface of the arguments that drive our conflicts and seek to examine the social dynamics at work. Drawing on some cultural studies (including ideology and political theory), I examine what drives people to come together and align themselves in groups against other groups, Christians against other Christians. I explore how this works against our life with God and against his mission.

Political theorists study what brings and holds people together. Likewise, thinkers in the field of ideology study what drives people to come together and how these drives shape them to do things and see themselves in certain ways. Sociologists conduct empirical studies of these dynamics in groups. In what follows, I outline some of the simplest ideas among these thinkers and ask how these very same dynamics work to shape the interminable conflicts among us.

By using some of these most basic concepts, I suggest we can diagnose some of our problems and better understand what drives our divisiveness. I also acknowledge that this kind of political therapy cannot solve our problems. For this, we must look to Scripture and to what God has indeed done in Christ. But perhaps we gain a few tools that can help us move beyond our current spiteful climate and then make space for God to work among us. Perhaps this can be a kind of therapy for our churches? And then we can go further. We can look to Scripture, in Christ, to shape a belief and practice that forms us as a people into the space beyond enemies, beyond the church of us vs. them. Let's take a look then at some of these tools and see where it leads us.

2

the enemy-making machine

Every church (and every other kind of group, for that matter) gathers around common beliefs. Beliefs hold a church together. Some beliefs are common to all Christians: "God the Father is Creator of heaven and earth," "Jesus is the Son of God," "He was crucified, died, and buried, and on the third day he arose again," and many other beliefs that are foundational to Christian life. But then there are distinctives that make churches different from each other. During the history of a church, a particular insight (into a doctrine, say) arises to help navigate a key moment in the life of the church. This insight rallies the church through challenging times and becomes an emphasis in the church's life. These distinctives are a normal part of being a church. What we do not see, however, is how these distinctives often form the basis for enemy making.

How do distinctives arise within a group? Sometimes it happens around a crisis among one group that then precipitates the starting of another group. For instance, when corruption in the medieval Catholic Church came to a boil in 1517 as priests were selling "indulgences" to lessen a person's punishment for sins in purgatory,

Martin Luther nailed his Ninety-Five Theses to the door of the Castle Church in Wittenberg. The corruption in the church led to a crisis. This afforded the space for Luther to articulate the insight "justification by faith alone" (not indulgences) as the basis for forgiveness and salvation. A distinctive was born: justification "by faith alone" and not "by the church and its control of the sacraments (and purgatory)." When the Catholic Church did not receive this new insight and change, a lot of people left to form a new church held together by this distinctive. This same pattern repeats throughout the history of the church within Christendom.

When alcoholism ran rampant among the peoples of Britain and across the frontiers of North America in the eighteenth and nineteenth centuries, the church was awakened to the toll it was taking on people's lives and neighborhoods. It saw a trauma and responded accordingly. Some preachers, influenced by the British preacher John Wesley, started calling for holiness. Others (often women) led temperance movements in their towns. They emphasized how Christians must continue on to live in the Spirit, give up alcohol, and be wholly sanctified. As they searched the Scriptures and listened to Wesley, they emphasized the belief in "entire sanctification." A great awakening happened among Christians in both Britain and North America as people were being delivered from alcohol problems. A distinctive (a new emphasis) was born that was peculiar to many groups of churches: entire sanctification (and various versions thereof). These churches formed denominations and were called "holiness churches" because they emphasized "holiness" and life in the Spirit.

Early in the twentieth century, the Industrial Revolution was destroying the lives of workers and their families. Hence arose another crisis. The large Euro-Protestant churches, which had many factory owners in their parishes, responded and preached that Christ had inaugurated the kingdom of God. He was Lord over the world and was indeed at work in the world. They called for a response to the worker crisis and for God's justice to be brought to fruition. Science, medicine, and democracy were all positives that were advances of the kingdom, they said. The church was to get out of its religious buildings and work for this kingdom in the world. Working for God's justice became a distinctive of (what we would later call) mainline Protestantism.

Other churches, of course, took a different approach. Some, for example, worried that this message of closely aligning the kingdom with modern science and politics was undermining the importance of Jesus himself bringing in the kingdom. These churches wanted to strongly affirm that Jesus would return in history to bring in the future kingdom. Reading Revelation 20:1–7, they preached that Jesus would come prior to the millennium and that only after this would the kingdom come. The message that he will return "after the gospel has been preached among all nations" (Matt. 24:14, my translation) became an impetus for missions and evangelism. Thus the distinctive of "premillenialism" was born, and those groups who gathered around this distinctive were deeply committed to Christ's second return and to world evangelism and mission.

In each of these moments, distinctives were born that marked a people as a group. These distinctives unified people around them and became central to the group's identity.[1] In each of the above cases, the group's distinctives started out as really important truths (or clarification of truths) that helped Christians navigate a social trauma, a crisis, a big cultural change they had to endure. But as these distinctives more and more became the reason the groups met, they became reified as (that is, made the permanent symbol of) the group's identity.

It's at this point that a conviction ("We don't drink alcohol") or a theological insight ("We depend on the Spirit for healing"; "Speaking in tongues is evidence of the filling of the Spirit") can, if we're not careful, take on a life of its own. "No drinking" becomes so central to the group's identity that members now begin to identify who's in the group (and who's not) by who doesn't drink (and who does). It acts less as a conviction worked out in every believer's life in response to a concrete issue and more as an identity marker—a symbol—of who we are and who's part of "us."

Whenever a distinctive belief becomes extracted from every-day life, from real-life discernment in the Spirit, and becomes an identity marker, it can be used to set up one side against another. It begins the process of enemy making. When a Methodist sees a friend getting drunk regularly in the early 1900s, he or she seeks to minister to the friend's possible alcoholism by bringing the gospel of total renewal to that person's life. A generation or two later, when the Methodists turn this insight into an identity marker, the Methodist sees a Christian drinking and perceives that person as backslidden or going to hell. The marker sets apart those who don't drink from those who do (especially those Lutherans who love their beer). It divides "us" against "them." Enemies are birthed. When this happens, the enemy-making machine sets into motion. Extracting beliefs from everyday life, making them a banner to be waved, creates enemies. It is the way the enemy-making machine works. It is the way ideology works.[2]

Today in North America, it's far more than drinking beer that divides. The enemy-making machine has crept into the church and created all sorts of new ideological markers that divide. Many churches are facing the horrors of racism in their neighborhoods and indeed their own churches for the first time. There's uncertainty over sexuality and gender in our culture. Immigrants of other religions are moving next door to Christians in our neighborhoods. We're facing new questions on social justice, witness, evangelism, and marriage that many of us have never faced before. These are real-life, concrete discernments in people's lives. We're discerning what God is saying in people's lives and in our neighborhoods. There are some stunning and helpful new insights for how to live in these tumultuous times. But often we take what we learned in one situation and apply it to a different situation, or without listening we make an assumption about another situation. Before we know it, we've turned an insight into a distinctive that rallies our church over against other churches that have made different discernments. Progressives get angry and impatient with conservatives, and vice versa. We shut off mutual discernment between Christians, and soon the enemy-making machine is running full throttle. And it works against everything God wants to do through Christ on the ground for his kingdom.

But the apostle Paul reminds the Corinthians that there can be no "I belong to Apollos" versus "I belong to Paul" (1 Cor. 3:4). For we are the "temple of God," and God by his Spirit "dwells" in us (1 Cor. 3:16). There can be no such antagonisms in his presence. Elsewhere Paul reminds the Corinthians that wherever Christ the Lord is present, "there is freedom" (2 Cor. 3:17). Wherever space is made for his presence, there can be no enslavement to the machine of strife, jealousy, or enemy making (v. 3). Instead, there is an openness to what he is doing. For "the glory of the Lord" is revealed here in this space of his presence. But wherever there is enemy making, as I will explain later, God cannot work for his purposes.

Is it possible to discern a good distinctive from an identity marker that makes enemies? Is there a way to keep good discernments in local churches from turning into boundary markers? Is there a way to put a wrench in the machinery of enemy making to make space for God's presence to work among us? When a distinctive that helps navigate circumstances in a church's life turns into a boundary marker, is there a way to reexamine and retranslate it faithfully for what that might mean in our actual lives and the context in which we live? Can the antagonisms be unwound so a people can submit to Christ and make space for Christ's manifest presence to be among us and remake our world?[3]

In what follows, playing off some theories of ideology and political theory, I explore some of the dynamics of the enemy-making machine.[4] What are the "tells" that reveal enemy making is

happening? What are some signs that the enemy-making machine
has been triggered? Like a good therapist, perhaps by knowing
these dynamics we can ask better questions and open space for
the living presence of Christ to be among us, working for healing,
transformation, and the renewal of all things.

Banners

As I said above, when distinctives become less about daily living
and more about what differentiates us from other people, they in
essence become banners to be waved around signaling who is in
and who is out of our group. What started out as good and helpful discernment in the life of a church becomes about marking
enemies. Whenever we extract a belief out of everyday practice, it
is a prime candidate for becoming a banner in the enemy-making
machine. You could say that "belief minus practice equals (almost
always) ideology." Cultural theorists have called these banners
"master signifiers."[5] Churches and leaders must learn how to discern when distinctives become master signifiers if we are ever to
avoid getting sucked into the enemy-making machine.

One sure "tell" that a distinctive has become a banner is that
it stops referring to anything real that affects how we live on a
day-to-day basis. Instead, it is now a symbol for who or what we
are against.

Recall, for instance, when then-candidate Barack Obama first
campaigned for president with the slogan "Change you can believe
in." He had been a community organizer in Chicago neighborhoods, so he knew what believing in change means to struggling
communities. As the distinctive was removed from community
organizing, however, and became a slogan of a national campaign,
it became a banner. The phrase did not link to anything he was
actually proposing. In fact, the strength of the slogan was that it
could mean different things to different people. Everyone hearing
the slogan could fill in what they thought it meant to their own

advantage. This is why cultural theorists call banners "master signifiers" or even "empty signifiers." They gather people around an idea that no longer has definite, concrete meaning. It does not refer to anything specific. Instead, people can fill that in themselves and rally around it.

"Change you can believe in" therefore meant different things to the white liberals in the north suburbs of Chicago, to struggling blue-collar workers in the steel mills of Gary, and to the African Americans who lived in communities on the south and west sides of Chicago. But people in all these groups could unite around voting for Barack Obama. They could bring a lot of energy to the cause. That was why it was such a good banner.

This same dynamic is repeated again and again in American politics. More recently we remember the Republican "Repeal and replace" slogan. Yet, when the time came, there actually was no substance behind it. The Republicans had no better plan with which to replace the Affordable Care Act. "Repeal and replace" became an empty signifier signaling to all Republicans that they were rallying against everything President Obama had stood for and accomplished in his eight years in office.

Some interpreted "Change you can believe in" as ABB: "Anything but (George) Bush." Indeed, the slogan did its best work rallying all kinds of people against a repeat of the George Bush Republicans. In the end, for many people, especially the more well-off economic classes, voting for Obama and displaying a bumper sticker made them feel good because they were for change and justice, but it cost them very little in terms of the privileges and affluence of their everyday lives. This is how ideology works. This is how things move in the enemy-making machine.

Distinctives can work the same way in churches. For instance, there are evangelical denominations today that hold premillennialism (see discussion in previous section) as a distinctive, despite the average member and most clergy no longer knowing what it means or how it might make a difference in the way they live the Christian life. It has become a banner. Seventy-five years of scholarship engaging the issue of the millennium (Rev. 20:1) rarely gets discussed. In some places, the premillennial belief is untouchable because it marks who we are and what we were once against. It drives our belief in world missions and evangelism. If we were to disrupt it or give it up, perhaps we'd lose our identity and ability to rally people to support the world missionary efforts and the budgets involved. So instead of deepening who we are in the Bible, it's quicker and easier just to hold on to the banner of premillennialism.

Banners get us excited about a cause and ignite us to put a lot of energy behind working against someone or something. But in the end, unfortunately, we end up spending so much energy rallying against an enemy that very little is left for actually living out these distinctives—like the affluent liberals who voted for Obama, about whom some wonder whether their victory left them with such a feeling of accomplishment that they had little energy left to change anything concrete in their daily lives. One has to wonder how much the "premillennial" banner has gathered Christians to support missions around the world even as it has allowed us to ignore the mission of God around our immediate neighborhoods.[6] Banners, as a rule, tend to make us passive toward actually living out our faith. They detach us from everyday life.

Not all distinctives turn into banners, but Christians need to be alert to banner making. We need to ask questions concerning what a particular banner means for how we as Christians actually live our lives. Banners are a main energy source for the enemy-making machine. Let us reject banners and instead seek to be faithful to practicing daily what we say we believe.

Enemies

A banner, as a general rule, rallies people against a group, an object, or a concept. That is part of its power to galvanize people around a cause. Having an enemy stokes the flames of anger and keeps the antagonism going. It's always easier to gather a group around what we're against, because it gets people angry. In this way, banners create enemies.

We discern whether a distinctive has become a banner by asking, Can this banner make sense apart from describing who or what the banner is against? If we can describe what we believe about the Bible only by first describing what people at the liberal church believe about the Bible, there's a good chance we are describing a banner. There may indeed be an important belief at stake. Nonetheless, if the banner only makes sense by describing what it is against, we must deconstruct this banner, dismantle it, and make space for God to work among us in this struggle.

A banner typically isolates an object that people can take aim at as the enemy. It is often a caricature of a kind of person or people group that becomes the enemy. This object we are against usually plays into a group's insecurities.[7] We may secretly envy the enemy and project onto him or her all the things that have gone wrong in our lives. We may even blame the enemy for our faults. Those who know World War II history remember how the Nazi ideology, which sought to defend the pure (*völkisch*) German culture, people, family, and lands, blamed the Jews for everything that undermined their German society. The Nazis projected greed, excess moneylending, and the weakening of German character onto "the Jew." But at the same time, the Nazis had a subliminal envy toward the Jews, who possessed what Hitler most wanted: a cohesive, pure race called to bless the nations (which for Hitler meant defeating them). It is perhaps the most horrific example of how our ideologies live off of the demonizing of an enemy through our making assumptions about them, taking out our worst insecurities on them, and trying to protect ourselves from them at all costs.

We see these extremes sometimes in our local church. Conservatives, for example, assume the worst about progressives and their

positions on sexuality. Likewise, progressives assume the worst
about any who question their conclusions regarding sexuality. Key
to breaking the hold of the enemy-making machine on our lives
is to probe what it is about the enemy that creates such fear, jealousy, envy, or even disgust in our lives. In looking at our enemies,
we always learn more about ourselves than about who we fight
against. In sitting with them, we open space for Christ's presence.

Perverse Enjoyment

We know that the enemy-making machine is turning its gears
when we sense a hint of glee inside ourselves at the sight of an
enemy failing or being defeated.[8] A telltale sign of this kind of
subtle "enjoyment" is when someone mutters beneath their breath,
"I'm sure glad I'm not one of them" (like the Pharisee in Luke
18:11) or "See, we're right after all." There's a strange sense of
vengeful satisfaction when we are proven right, a certain sense of
security that comes at the expense of someone outside the group.
I now feel more secure in my own beliefs and place in life because
of the other side's failure, and I'm feeling good about it. This is
profoundly non-Christian. All of this perverse enjoyment is a sure
sign we've been caught in the enemy-making machine.

The appearance of vengeful glee in my life is a clue to how
much my identity has become part of the enemy-making machine.[9]
I am not aware of how much my passions and attractions have
been shaped by my allegiance to the group. My reason for living
has become attached to this cause. My sense of who I am, even
my location and role in life, has been found in this group and the
cause of defeating this enemy. It is so much a part of who I am
that it is now impossible for someone to directly dialogue with
me about my position. Direct evidence that I am in fact wrong is
irrelevant, because for me to give up my position is to throw my
very self into chaos. But occasionally the excesses of my enjoyment at someone else's demise reveal the emptiness behind the

enemy-making machine—if someone can just be with me long enough to help me see it.

By its nature, this perverse enjoyment is not recognized by the group. No one says such things out loud. Because it is reprehensible to express such things, these enjoyments are generally repressed, which in turn allows the subjects to remain locked into the ideological force of the group. We keep coming back to the meetings to enjoy small victories, all the while feigning empathy for the other side's grief. It's all part of the enemy-making machine.

After the 9/11 attacks on New York City, the images of the planes piercing the Twin Towers were burned into our imaginations as news channels repeatedly replayed them. With this arose an intense reverence and patriotism, and with it a self-gratifying sense that we are not like those Islamic fundamentalists who do not believe in freedom and respect for every individual. The "Islamic fundamentalist" became stereotyped as the enemy. Freedom became the banner around which we all united in a war against terror. In the face of horrific loss, we almost perversely enjoyed the feeling that we were the greatest, bravest, most free nation on earth.

During that time after 9/11, our church met on Sunday nights to pray for peace, healing, reconciliation. On one of those Sunday nights, I asked those who were gathered for prayer, What do you think God would have us do as a church in response to the 9/11 attacks? I talked about praying for discernment for our government, people afraid to fly or do business, and the many Muslims in our neighborhoods afraid to leave their homes. One of the men stood up, smiled, and declared, "I believe God has one thing for us to do: to go kick some a** and teach these people a lesson." Surprisingly, some of our people said "Amen!" rather loudly. This vengeance brought him, and others in the congregation, a sense of excitement, even enjoyment. The enemy-making machine plays on this feeling. It keeps it going. Sometimes we have to provoke the expression of such glee so we can ask questions and reveal the contradictions at work. It's all part of breaking the spell of its power over us.

Some claimed that church attendance went up 25 percent in the United States in the months following 9/11. And with this, church leaders announced that we're turning back to God during this time of crisis. However, just a few short months later church attendance had already returned to pre-9/11 levels. What was driving the intensity of that surge in church attendance? And why did it not last?

The church can only sustain its existence via the enemy-making machine by continually making new enemies, creating more fear and desire for vengeance toward an object. Jesus, on the other hand, challenges his disciples to love their enemies, to be with people. The apostle Paul urged Christians to weep with those who weep. This is the kind of presence God will use to change the world. But it is ever thwarted by the enemy-making machine. It is only possible by opening up space to be with those we disagree with, trusting Jesus is Lord and working among us.

Antagonism

Banners always promise something in the future to those who will join the cause. Like the banner of freedom after 9/11 or of the spread of the gospel to all the nations before the millennium will come, banners are kept going by their future promises. When these promises prove elusive, we have an enemy to blame, whether the "Islamic fundamentalist" who wants to destroy our freedom or the "mainline liberal" who doesn't believe in missions anymore. And this us vs. them approach stokes the energy around our distinctives that keeps us going as a group. It's the way of antagonism.[10] It's the way ideology works. It keeps the enemy-making machine going.

The drive to work together against an enemy toward the unfulfilled promise often leads to contradictions between what we say and what we do.[11] Although the banner doesn't mean what we thought it meant, we don't care. Because we are more invested in what we are against, we often end up doing things that contradict what we say we believe. Sometimes the best thing we can do with people caught in the enemy making machine is to sit with them, asking questions about the contradictions and how these are working for the person.

After 9/11, the Patriot Act was passed within a matter of weeks, authorizing a host of new abilities of government agencies to detain immigrants and search homes, business records, internet sites, and cell phone communications. We were willing to give up our freedoms in the name of freedom, the banner under which we were doing these things. The thinking was that we must do whatever was needed to defeat the enemy, "those Islamic fundamentalist terrorists." Few were willing to ask advocates of these policies questions that revealed the contradictions.

Allowing our lives to be determined by what we are against, and by the fear and anger that accompanies it, defeats what God might be doing in the conflict itself. Because we are blinded by our single-minded focus on the enemy being defeated, we cannot see how God works between people in their disagreements. So we must resist participating in the antagonisms. We can start by asking good questions that reveal the contradictions. As we sit before the person condemning all Islamic terrorists, we remember that God does not wish anyone to perish (2 Pet. 3:9) and that he did not come to condemn the world but to heal the world (John 3:17). If we can but irenically disrupt this machine for a short moment, we might then open space to be present one to another, the space for Christ's presence to become manifest between us and our Muslim neighbors. Perhaps we might then have the room to discern what God is doing in our midst. This is the space "beyond enemies."

Beyond Enemies: The Caffeine Free Diet Coke

The cultural theorist Slavoj Žižek uses the Caffeine Free Diet Coke as a metaphor for the way ideology works. It is a metaphor for what happens to Christians and the church when taken over by the enemy-making machine.

According to Žižek, prior to World War I, Coca-Cola was a medicine (known as a nerve tonic, stimulant, and headache remedy). Then, during Prohibition, it was sweetened to make its strange taste more palatable, and it became a popular drink to replace alcohol because of its stimulant qualities (it was deemed "refreshing" as well as the perfect "temperance drink"). Then, in its modern version, its sugar was replaced with artificial sweetener and its caffeine was extracted to take out health-negative ingredients. What we are left with is Caffeine Free Diet Coke.

Today, therefore, Caffeine Free Diet Coke has become a drink that does not quench thirst and does not provide any stimulant effects and whose strange taste is not particularly satisfying. Nonetheless it is one of the most consumed beverages in the world. There's a mysterious enjoyment we get out of consuming it after we have already quenched our thirst with something else. "Coke is 'it'" not because it satisfies any material need. In essence, all that remains in Caffeine Free Diet Coke of what was once Coke is an artificial promise of a substance that never materializes. In Žižek's words, we "drink nothing in the guise of something."[12]

Taking some liberties with Žižek's illustration, Caffeine Free Diet Coke can also make for a good metaphor to understand how the enemy-making machine works to empty the church of who we are as Christ's people. Our core beliefs, such as the Bible as God's Word, salvation in Christ, and the church as God's people for mission, can become banners we wave that define us as Christians over against other people or groups. Yet in the process, these beliefs are emptied of their substance as we disciple each other in the course of everyday life. They are ideological banners that we assent to but that bear little or no connection to our lives in Christ for his mission in the world. Just as our society drinks Coke as "it," as something that makes us feel good but has little substantial value as a drink, so we practice these beliefs as something we add on to our lives—not as something that shapes the way we live and the kinds of people we are. Like drinking a Caffeine Free Diet Coke, Christianity becomes something we do as part of our already busy lives, something that makes us feel better but changes little. This is what the enemy-making machine does to church.

As we are drawn in to the antagonisms of making enemies, we become separated from the reality of what our life is all about in Christ. The beliefs we have held for years no longer mean anything for how we actually live our lives. We are a facsimile that runs on angry, defensive energy. The enemy-making machine shapes the church to be a facade of what an actual church should be. In other words, we are empty at the core.

Church done this way over the years wears us out because it drains our energy and the joy of the life God has given us. We may sing songs, preach, and help the poor, but we sing our particular songs as opposed to those who don't, and we preach the Word while those churches across the street and around the corner don't, and we help the poor because we're better than those who don't. Our life as God's people is empty inside because there is nothing of the fullness of Christ's presence to fill our daily lives in the kingdom among the world.[13] And because we are defensive and antagonistic in our being, we cannot invite anyone into what God is doing among us. Our witness becomes void of reality. We know what we're against, but we have forgotten what we are for.

It's Time

If you remember Justin's story at the beginning of the previous chapter, he was a man torn by insecurities in a changing world. He was angry and hopeless at the same time. He had very little to hold on to except to respond to others as his enemy. The problem of Justin is the problem of the church in present-day North America. Amid massive changes in our culture since the 2016 election, we have simmering antagonisms running at the core of our lives. We are defensive. We are driven by insecurities. The antagonisms of the church keep us going. But we have little to offer the world in terms of transformation, healing, and renewal.

The challenge before us is to dig deep, to look carefully at the distinctives that characterize our lives together in our churches—to ask why the defensiveness (how are they an enemy?), to challenge the vengeful glee (where is that coming from?), to unwind the antagonisms (who has sinned and how do we forgive/receive forgiveness?)—so that we can make space for Christ to be present among us and work in the world. Here in his presence, his kingdom can become visible. But the antagonisms must be unwound first.

We could of course start by examining today's most controversial issues: the church's stance on sexuality in the past ten years, the church's response to racism, and the culture's pluralism of religions. But I propose we start with our most central beliefs and the way they have (at times) been turned into antagonisms. I contend that the Bible, conversion, and the church's engagement of social justice have somehow been caught up in the enemy-making machine. Instead of being the foundation of the way we live our lives as Christians, these beliefs and practices now undermine how we live as Christians. I'm convinced that learning how to discern God's Word together, practice discipleship, and engage injustice in his presence (as opposed to antagonism) equips us to navigate the contentious issues of our times in a space that is beyond enemies.

And so, in what follows, I show how each one of these beliefs has been caught up in the enemy-making machine. I then describe the practice of what God has given us in the Bible, salvation, and the church that counters this enemy making. Instead of us vs. them, we practice each belief in his presence for the world. For everything profoundly changes when we practice discerning God's Word together, discipleship, and engagement with injustice in the space of his presence beyond enemies. He is able to make forgiveness real, convict of sin, reconcile, heal, renew, and transform. This first happens among us as his body, the church. And then we are able to enter the antagonisms of the world in the same way, opening space for his healing, reconciling presence in the world. To this work we now turn.

3

are you biblical?

It's Sunday morning in Houston and eighteen thousand people have gathered for worship at Lakewood Church. Pastor Joel Osteen steps to the mic and begins his sermon by asking everyone to raise their Bibles high and repeat these words:

> This is *my* Bible.
> I am what it says I am.
> I can do what it says I can do.
> Today, I will be taught the Word of God.
> I boldly confess:
> My mind is alert, My heart is receptive.
> I will never be the same.
> I am about to receive
> The incorruptible, indestructible,
> Ever-living seed of the Word of God.
> I will never be the same.
> Never, never, never.
> I will never be the same.
> In [Jesus's] name. Amen.[1]

Thousands of black Bibles are hoisted in the air across the congregation. It all epitomizes how the Bible is the center of the church's gathering. The Bible is "the incorruptible, indestructible, Ever-living seed." It symbolizes just how much Protestants believe that the Bible carries ultimate authority for the Christian.

And yet many Bible-centered Christians see Osteen and his church as a poor example of practicing biblical authority. Prominent church leaders like Al Mohler Jr., Mark Driscoll, and Denny Burk have accused Osteen, at various times, of spurious interpretation of the Bible. He preaches heresy ("prosperity gospel"), they say. All of these people, including Osteen, adhere to the Bible's authority over their lives. Yet somehow the Bible, which should gather Christians in unity, becomes the tool that divides Christians from one another. It gets sucked into the enemy-making machine. How does this happen?

There Was a Time

From the church's very beginnings, the Scriptures have played a central role in its life. The apostle Paul quoted (what is now) the Old Testament as he wrote his letters to the churches of the first century. He explained the gospel "according to" the Scriptures. He claimed the Old Testament—the only form of the Bible that he had at the time—as "God-breathed" (2 Tim. 3:16 NIV).[2] This thinking later extended to the New Testament canon. The church fathers of the second, third, and fourth centuries quoted, explained, and preached the books of both Testaments. If we consider the writings of Augustine, Anselm, Luther, Calvin, Menno Simons, John Wesley, and Jonathan Edwards, these leaders of the Western church all used the Bible as the primary source of authority for the church, its people, and its leadership.[3] And so, it seems, there was a time when the Bible gathered people around its authority instead of divided them.

For sure there were differences in interpretation between these people. But the church had a teaching office that eventually unified the church's interpretation. Whether it was the apostles of the early church or the councils and synods of the church fathers and the popes, there were systems that brought people together around the authority of the Bible.

When the Reformation came, the church was in conflict in Europe. And Luther famously challenged the pope based on Scripture. Several years later, a series of religious wars broke out in Europe over various interpretations of Scripture, among other things. Some suggest these wars were political wars over control of wealth and territory. Interpretations of various doctrines were used for this end.[4] Nonetheless, despite the fighting, people still generally believed that the Bible carried supreme authority within the church.

Today, however, strife over the Bible has taken on a whole new dynamic, and it threatens our witness before the world. Something has changed about our approach to the Bible, living as we do in a culture that no longer assumes the Bible is true. In the church, it is now the belief itself in the authority of the Bible—and who gets to interpret it and how—that we fight over.

We remember Justin, who was raised in a rural town where no one questioned the Bible's authority in his small circle of church friends. Even the "liberal" church in town considered it heresy to question the Bible's authority in a Christian's life. But once Justin got to the "big city," he met people who did not care so much about the Bible and considered it an ancient artifact. Then there were those who did believe the Bible but could not agree on several matters of interpretation of the Bible. And so Justin found himself in a new moment where he was forced to defend his allegiance to the Bible in ways he never had to before. He was forced to answer questions like, Why do I obey Scripture? How do I know which parts to obey? Just like Justin did, the church today finds itself in this new moment. It has been forced to think about the Bible differently in a secularized (post-Christendom) world. The authority of Scripture is threatened by the presence of a new audience that no longer automatically believes in the authority of the Bible.

The Trauma

This new moment did not arrive all at once. Some of it can be traced to the 1920s (and earlier) in North America. This was a time when leaders in American seminaries and churches were adopting a new method of study called the historical-critical method. Instead of reading the Bible as a sacred text, they read it according to the rules that shaped how any other historical document would be read in the universities. These preachers and scholars were called "modernists."[5]

As this modernist thinking reached popular, everyday church life, it seemed that preachers and leaders were now questioning things that had been accepted for hundreds of years. They were challenging the historical accuracy of the creation story, the flood narrative, Jesus's virgin birth, his miracles, and even the resurrection, because these biblical events supposedly did not pass the tests used to confirm the historical reliability of other ancient texts. Books were published announcing the Bible was full of historical and scientific inaccuracies. Christians everywhere were up in arms. It was like the Bible was a rug of security that was being pulled out from beneath them.

A defensive reaction was set into motion. Conservative leaders—known as "fundamentalists"—responded with efforts to defend the truthfulness of the Scriptures (and the beliefs that were rooted in them). They wrote books. They had conferences. They fought against the liberal ideas from Germany that were supposedly undermining the gospel truth of the Bible. In return, famous liberal preacher Harry Emerson Fosdick fought back and preached a sermon at his Presbyterian church in New York titled "Shall the Fundamentalists Win?" In it he argued that the church does not need a virgin birth, the miracles of Jesus, or the Bible as God's error-free Word in order to sustain its Christian faith. For Fosdick, all we needed was to follow the Spirit of Christianity. Philanthropist John D. Rockefeller Jr. loved the sermon and published 130,000 copies to be distributed to Protestant clergymen everywhere. A major disruption was happening in the churches.

Around this time, Princeton Seminary scholar B. B. Warfield wrote the essays that became *The Inspiration and Authority of the Bible*. In them he defended the Bible's authority based on the idea that the Bible itself claims to be divinely verbally inspired by the Holy Spirit. Second Timothy 3:16 said unabashedly that all Scripture is "God-breathed." It was a clear and logical conclusion: If the Bible is "God-breathed," it must be inerrant. It must be without error, whether historical, scientific, or otherwise. And so the inerrancy defense was born and proved to be very helpful to Christians of this time who were working to sort out the Bible's authority in the age of modern science.[6]

As the inerrancy defense became popular among pastors, many church denominations adopted inerrancy as a doctrinal statement to assure parishioners that their leadership believed in the Bible. As Fosdick and others pushed back, saying that science contradicted the Bible, Christian leaders were forced to choose between the authority of Scripture and the discoveries of science. Denominations were split between those who adopted the new creed of inerrancy and those who believed in science. Bible institutes and Bible conferences were formed. A whole movement of churches named "_____ Bible Church" sprang up across the land. The doctrine of inerrancy shaped a whole new politics of the church. For many, an assent to inerrancy symbolized that they weren't "one of those liberals."

Today, many years later, the actual belief in inerrancy is less prominent among Christians, but Protestants (on both sides of the issue) in North America are still determined by it. The oft-quoted quip "The Bible says it, I believe it, and that settles it for me" was first used to assert the Bible's authority over against the liberals in the 1920s. Likewise, in the 1960s, Billy Graham's "The Bible says!" was his assertion of belief in the Bible amid those who would doubt its veracity.[7] Few remember that in the 1970s John Osteen, Joel's father, developed the confession that opened this chapter amid the inerrancy debates of that day. Each statement in its own way was a reassertion of biblical authority in the midst of the modernist attacks by mainline liberals.

Conservative scholar Harold Lindsell published *The Battle for the Bible*, which became a bestseller in 1978 and rallied thousands to stay armed against the "slippery slope" toward denying the Bible's inerrancy. Books like Josh McDowell's *Evidence That Demands a Verdict* and Lee Strobel's *The Case for Christ* became bestsellers arguing for the scientific veracity of the Bible, among other things. Those of us who grew up reading these books and others like them were being trained to defend the Bible. Meanwhile, mainline liberals and progressive evangelicals looked down on these books with an intellectual superiority. Subtly, with few even noticing, the enemy-making machine was getting revved up around the belief in inerrancy that was shaping Christians in North America.

Years later, the trauma of the "inerrant Bible" haunts the ways both sides think about and practice reading the Bible. Evangelical conservatives and Protestant liberals are caught up in the residuals left over by these battles, arguing in a cycle via patterns of biblical interpretation based on things like authorial intent, lexicography, grammar, and Jewish and Greco-Roman backgrounds. And it has produced an echo chamber that, while it might provide an occasional insight, rarely gets us anywhere in discerning how to live the Christian life and engage the injustices of the world.

Like the car dealers from the introduction of this book, operating in a world where people no longer value cars, we continue to fight over whose car is the best, what its best features are, and how each car gives the best driver experience. Meanwhile, the world has moved on, and people are getting their rides from self-driving

autonomous vehicles owned by Uber. We've made the Bible a cause
to get behind, a belief to be argued over, a battleground on which
to wage war—and in the process the Bible has lost its place among
us as that which shapes our lives into Christ and his presence and
mission in and for the world.

The Banner of the "Inerrant Bible"

The "inerrant Bible" has many qualities that make for a good banner. Remember, for instance, that a good banner doesn't actually
refer to anything in real life. It's a concept that people can rally
around, but it costs them very little in terms of actually having
to change anything in their day-to-day lives. Inerrancy is a belief
that works this way.

Notice, for instance, that when "inerrancy" is used in an organization's belief or mission statement, it is often accompanied by the
phrase "according to the original autographs."[8] This dates back to
the doctrine as first written by Warfield himself.[9] It acknowledges
that there could have been errors in the transmission of the texts
of the Bible from the original documents to the latest documents
we have at the present time, which means the Bible's inerrancy can
only be guaranteed as it applies to the original documents. But of
course no one has ever located or seen the original manuscripts,
nor is there any real hope of that happening. And so the phrase
"according to the original autographs" is a clue that "inerrant
Bible" is really more of a symbol than an actual reality. Even if it
rarely happens, the possibility exists that we can argue away any
historical error on the basis of its being a redaction, a later addition, or an error in transmission. The fact that there are errors in
the Bible thus becomes somewhat irrelevant. Yet inerrancy as a
banner does serve to indicate who the true believers in the Bible
are: they are those who believe in inerrancy.

Perhaps more importantly, the banner of the inerrant Bible
does little to inform how Christians live out the actual truths of

Scripture. Simply affirming the Bible as inerrant gives the impression that the person gives authority to the Bible, but this seems to ignore how the person is actually interpreting the text. And so organizations and their leaders, from places as divergent as Osteen's Lakewood Church in Houston, Moody Bible Institute, Compassion International, the Billy Graham Association, and Willow Creek Community Church, all affirm a version of "divinely inspired," "infallible" or "inerrant," and "according to the original autographs." And yet they teach things, promote lifestyles and values, and organize discipleship practices that are vastly different from one another. But still somehow, under the inerrancy banner, each individual's or organization's or church's allegiance to the inerrant Bible symbolizes "evangelical" orthodoxy.

This is how the enemy-making machine starts up. It gathers people around a banner—the Bible is true!—but the banner actually demands nothing specific from us in terms of how we live. Worse, the banner may end up distracting its adherents from reading the Bible more carefully and discerning our faithfulness to following Jesus. We spend more time defending the Bible than reading it. The banner becomes the means to energize us against someone else—those liberals who see historical errors in the Bible!—and then keeps us busy working for the cause against those other people. But in the process, we are distracted from actually reading the Bible together, from submitting our lives to Jesus, who by the Spirit might teach us together through the reading of the Bible. This is all part of the subtle, insidious way the enemy-making machine works.

On What It (Really) Means to Be "Biblical"

Few churchgoers today talk much about inerrancy. Instead, other banners that do essentially the same thing have taken its place. For example, notice how the word "biblical" is used among Christians.[10] This word is one of the most used words among Protestant evangelical churches. It is short for saying "What I have just said can be defended directly out of the inspired Bible, chapter and verse." And yet, often there is no actual referent to the Bible given to back up the claim. When a Bible verse is given, there is no acknowledgment that the interpretation being espoused needs to be examined, that there are indeed other interpretations. "Biblical," therefore, is often an empty signifier. In other words, it really doesn't mean what it says: that what was just said is indisputably backed by the Bible. Instead it is much more slippery when actually put into practice. Often it can just be a term for something we as a church generally accept as Christian. But using the word "biblical" just gives more authority to whatever the thing is.

In the churches I grew up in, the word "biblical" had a strange power to gain the higher moral ground on any issue that was in dispute, even when those who used it hadn't worked through the hermeneutics of a particular text. When disagreements would flare, a leader in the room could stand up, sometimes recite a biblical text (with no attempt to interpret it), and simply declare his or her position "biblical." Then a bunch of people would nod their heads, say "of course!" and that side would gain leverage in the debate. Behind this rhetorical maneuver lies the belief in an inerrant Bible where texts are inspired and the meaning is therefore assumed to be self-evident.

Likewise today, "biblical" is a power word in many churches. Its use can cut short a conversation as the so-called expert in the Bible, who alone has the authority to interpret it, exerts one position over another as orthodox. And there is a subtext: if you disagree with "biblical," you can be marked as not biblical (or less biblical), as a "liberal"—and nobody wants to be labeled as such.

This is what a banner does. It forces people to choose sides quickly. It creates an enemy, the "liberal" who is not biblical, and then makes the people who disagree into an "other." It sets into motion an antagonism that will ensnare everyone in its clutches. It sets up the church to be us vs. them. As a result, the church, caught up in the banner's antagonism, bypasses real life on the ground with people who wish to discern life by reading the Bible together and asking, What is God calling us to engage for the gospel?

If we are to ever lead Christians to the space beyond enemies, where Christ becomes present and works, we must question banners that organize the enemy-making machine like this. As soon as we see that a belief has little to do with actual discipleship but is only organizing us against someone, we must ask good questions: What do you actually mean when you say _____? How have you experienced that in your own life? When someone says a position is biblical, we can ask: What text are you referring to? What do you do with this particular interpretation that disagrees with what you're saying? Can we study this more closely together?

Asking questions humbly, with grace and invitation, makes space for Christ's presence to work among us. Jesus does this all the time.[11] He is present in the asking of a good question with humility and gentleness. Let us ask questions that probe the emptiness behind the banner. Good questions can disrupt the antagonism and open space for God to work among us through reading the Bible. Remember: this is what Jesus often did with the Pharisees, who sought to control conversations and get the high ground. He made space for people to be listened to, for the person's real situation to be acknowledged in his presence.

The Excess and Glee of Bumper Sticker Battles

Excessive expressions of enjoyment at another person's expense sound the alarm that the enemy-making machine is running at full throttle. As mentioned in the previous chapter, the pleasure behind this enjoyment is what keeps people locked into the antagonism. It is the way ideology works.

The February 2014 Ham/Nye debates over creation science caused quite a fuss in the media. Creation scientist Ken Ham debated Bill Nye, the "Science Guy" from popular television, over whether creation had a proper basis in science. At the core of Ham's work is the defense of a literal seven-day creation and a "young Earth," because this is what the book of Genesis and the genealogies of the Old Testament teach. Ham argues for these truths based on every word of the Bible being inerrant (creation in seven literal days) and historically accurate (genealogies tied to a young Earth time frame) because it is God's Word, God-breathed.[12]

The debate itself was rather pedestrian, but the response was stunning. NPR reported that more than 500,000 people watched it live and another 830,000 viewed it on YouTube within a few days. Local churches had viewing parties. The size of the audience was unprecedented for a debate. The ensuing debate over who won the debate lasted for days on social media and in online publications and journals.[13] Many on the cable news networks thought Bill Nye had won, but it was irrelevant.[14] The debate likely changed few minds; it just got people on each side more energized to cheer on their own side. None of this is surprising, because this is the way the enemy-making machine works.

People enjoy taking the other side down. A T-shirt that became popular among teenagers read "I believe in the big-bang theory. God spoke and BANG it happened." Bumper stickers that said "Evolution is a theory. Creation is a fact" started showing up on cars. The other side's favorite bumper sticker depicted a stick figure of a fish—the symbol of Christianity—with feet, suggesting fish evolving into land creatures. Both sides played an endless game of who could develop the snarkiest bumper sticker. One side said, "I learned everything I needed to know about evolution at the Holocaust." The other side said, "I went to the Creation Museum and all I got was stupid." A virtual bumper sticker industry emerged to mock creationism.

The Ham/Nye debate was held at the Creation Museum. Built in 2007 at a cost of $27 million, the museum had Disneyesque aspirations. It displayed scientific arguments that defend the seven-day creation/young-Earth creationism account with theme park–like productions. In its first ten years, the museum drew 2.5 million visitors. The day it opened, scientists, educators, students, and atheists protested at a "Rally for Reason" organized by Edwin Kagin of American Atheists.

Meanwhile, through it all, one wonders whether the beauty of the knowledge of God as Creator is lost amid the arguments. Indeed, for many inerrantists, wouldn't an actual literal reading of Genesis 1–3 require that we take its poetic features into account in understanding it as history? Doesn't "Adam" in Hebrew literally mean "humanity" (it's true meaning is metaphoric) and is not "the tree of life" a poetic metaphor describing the life-giving source at the core of the garden? Does not this account point in depth to God's love and purpose in creating all of creation? And yet so much of this is lost in the glee over winning an argument—lost too is our witness to the onlooking world. If we are to ever inhabit a place that is beyond enemies, we surely must make space among real people who are caught up in the excess glee, and we must ask, Why are we so energized at the thought of taking down our enemies? Then, amid the calm, we can sort out what this has to do with the God we worship and the work he is doing to transform the world.

The Bible as Blunt Instrument

Even though inerrancy has drifted off the consciousness of many Christians in the twenty-first century, its influence persists. For many, the hold of literal interpretation of every biblical text as "God-breathed" drives how the Bible is used at the point of conflict. As such, the Bible often turns into an arsenal of inspired verses cherry-picked to wage war against the opposition on any given topic. What we used to call the "inerrant Bible" laid the foundation for making the Bible the basis for this kind of oppositional logic. It's the enemy-making machine doing what it does best.

The process usually begins with "conservatives," those most influenced in their past by inerrancy, choosing the right verses to make their point. Then those who question the position—let's call them "progressives" (often ex-conservative evangelicals)— get pulled into the same hermeneutic trying to prove those verses don't mean what the other side says they mean. And we're off! The notion of an inerrant Bible becomes woven into the antagonism and keeps it going.

An example of this is the conflict over gay and lesbian sexuality within today's churches. Typically, the traditional side of the conflict seeks to prove that same-sex sexuality is wrong by citing several texts in the Bible. Each text is inspired. Specific texts are selected that speak about gay sexuality, and these are strung together to make the case that the Bible declares same-sex sexuality is wrong. These texts are usually very explicit about same-sex sexual relations, especially the passages from Leviticus. And so it is very clear from the Bible, they say, that gay and lesbian sexuality is a sin.

At first glance, this approach makes excellent sense. Christians seek guidance from the Bible, the full authority of which they proclaim. When we disagree about a particular issue, we should find verses that talk about the issue and use these to make our case.

But this sets into motion the return response on the same terms. The exact same way that the Bible is used to make the conservatives' argument is used to make counterarguments by the progressive side. The texts are treated one at a time, because each text is individually inspired. The progressive scholars argue that, in the case of Paul and the Old Testament, these texts refer to a kind of sexuality that has nothing to do with today's understanding of long-term, committed gay and lesbian relationships. Locked into the same "inerrant" Bible logic, the entirety of the debate hinges on what the Bible verses actually mean when they talk about sodomy and lust. Then, similarly, scholars from this side ask why we use texts like Leviticus 18:22 and 20:13 as normative on sexuality while other texts—such as those about stoning a woman who cannot prove her virginity before marrying (Deut. 22:20–21) or punishing the man who touches a woman within seven days after menstruation (Lev. 15:19)—are ignored. One side argues, "We have more than 31,000 verses in the Bible; not a single one of them has a positive thing to say about homosexual relationships."[15] The other side argues that there are only seven texts in the entire Bible that address the issue: "Compare that to the more than 250 verses on the proper use of wealth or more than 300 on our responsibility to care for the poor."[16] The seven texts that are most used against same-sex sexuality are now sometimes referred to as the "clobber passages," because they are used to clobber gay and lesbian people.[17] Meanwhile, the Bible as the story of the unfolding of God's salvation in the world, including God's redemption and healing of sexuality, is lost. Instead of being a narrative exposition of God's mission, of what he is doing, how he works, and what he is calling us into, it has become a blunt weapon, stripped of its true power, used to antagonize and to make points and win.

Ironically, as we shall see in the next chapter, this is not being true to the character of the Bible itself, which is much more than a book of propositional scientific texts. Caught up in the logic of inerrancy, though, even when neither side has a clear sense of what "inerrant" might mean, the Bible becomes a tool of the enemy-making machine. And people outside Christianity who look at us just shake their heads and wonder why people would shape their moral lives around an ancient text taken literally.[18] Popular atheists look on and say, "These stupid Christians! They take literally the Bible that justifies trafficking in humans, ethnic cleansing, slavery, bride-price, and indiscriminate massacre."[19] And based on that, they reject (or accept) gay marriage? Meanwhile, the atheists adopt the same reading strategy of the conservatives/progressives for the Bible and decide on that basis they must reject it entirely.

But the Bible is God's Grand Drama unfolding in time and history. It is God overcoming the sin, pain, brokenness, and violence of the world. It is the one true story we are invited to discern and enter into, to participate in via his presence and power in our lives. But in our infighting, it is completely lost to us and the world. In our enemy making, we lose the Bible as the means by which we come together, read, and then bow before the God at work among us and in the world. Our means for discerning what God is actually doing among us, his healing and redeeming work, is bypassed and ignored. Instead, the Bible is used to shape the church into a place of us vs. them. This is what the enemy-making machine does.

The Kinds of People We Become

I remember attending a large church in Chicago back when I was single. We would gather every Sunday night for an hour to hear what was called expository preaching. The pastor taught by going through a Bible passage verse by verse, paying careful attention to what each word meant in the original languages. Each night, there would be one or two applications for our lives that would come from the text. Then my friends and I would go out afterward to a Chicago establishment and enjoy each other's presence.

As time went on it became noticeable how many of us could not wait for the church service to end. There was little connection between the Bible and our lives. We were learning the Bible cognitively. We were taking good notes. We were learning much *about* the Bible, but we were not discerning the Bible in relation to our everyday lives and God's living presence working among us. We were parsing it. And when we got to the restaurant each night after the service ended, it was like the teaching had never happened. It had not connected. We weren't arguing over the Bible during those times, but we also weren't particularly attached to the Bible. It had lost its power to be used by the Spirit to illumine our lives as to who God was and how he was present in our lives. The Bible was inerrant but meant nothing to us in the day-to-day stuff of living our lives with God.

To me, this illustrates what it looks like when people have been caught up in the enemy-making machine in their use of the Bible. The Bible becomes an object to be defended and studied for truth, but in the process we have forgotten to be present to God and his presence among us as we read and study the Bible together. Instead, God has become truth to be learned conceptually from the Bible and even defended on the basis of the Bible. Jesus—the revealed Son of God, majestic Lord of the world, sovereign King of the universe revealing himself to us in history and in our very lives—had been lost from our consciousness.

One of the first Bible studies I attended in Chicago in my thirties was with a group of men from one of the larger churches in the city. It was obvious we were all struggling with issues in our lives. We were studying the book of John using inductive Bible study guides that would lead us verse by verse to ask questions and fill in answers. Who was the author of John's Gospel? Was it John the disciple? What did these words mean? One night a very curious nonbeliever came to the Bible study. He questioned why we cared so much about what the Bible said. We said that it was true; it was God's Word. An animated discussion began. The visitor questioned some of our facts. But then, after we had firmly defended our position, he asked, "What difference does it make in your life?" He said to us, "You all seem as conflicted and miserable as people I know who don't believe the Bible." In the ensuing weeks, we realized that for months we had been meeting, and we had studied words carefully, but we could not point to one deep discussion we had had about our lives, our circumstances. We could not tell our visitor one example of how this Bible study had opened our eyes to Christ's work among us or led us to submit to him with our lives. We had been studying a historical text but avoiding our lives.

This is the way ideology (as I have defined it) works. It distracts us from actual on-the-ground living. It draws us into feelings, desires, and antagonisms that take on a life of their own. Because our lives do not reflect what we're actually talking about, it destroys our witness.

On Becoming Arrogant People

For many of us, the "inerrant Bible" has become a banner that shapes our imagination, how we relate to people, and the kinds of people we have become in the world. For others, years after "inerrancy" has passed from our vernacular, it still shapes the way we read the Bible. We no longer read the Bible to immerse ourselves in the world where Jesus is Lord. We no longer read the Bible together to discern his work in our lives and all around us. We have become defined by what we believe about the Bible rather than how we live our lives as an extension of the Bible.

In my early forties, my wife and I moved to the northwest suburbs of Chicago to plant what would become Life on the Vine Church. In that first year I must have had coffee with over two hundred people talking about the possibility of a new church presence in the northwest burbs. I went to each Starbucks, McDonald's, or local coffeehouse with the goal of being present with people who were interested in making way for a new church presence in our suburb. I wanted to hear what God was doing in their lives, what it meant for them to participate in God's kingdom, and discern whether God was calling them to enter this new community of the kingdom of God or to continue to help in their original church's life and mission. I'd ask, "Do you see the need for a new witness to God's kingdom here? Can you discern God's call to this mission?" I wanted to open space and see what God was doing in them. This is the only way it made sense for me to engage people about kingdom formation in our suburb.

Nine times out of ten—I do not exaggerate—the conversation would turn to a horror story about what had happened to the person in previous church experiences. Church planters tend to connect with people who have had bad experiences in their previous church. To me, these experiences were telling. They would say things like, "I was told I was evil for questioning the Bible." "I was excommunicated from the church because I dared to talk about my sexual issues having to do with same-sex attraction." "I felt ostracized by my church during my darkest hour of getting a divorce." "I dared question a leader on how we spent money and I was asked to leave my church." Each time, the Bible was used to judge and exclude people who did not line up with the leader's specific take on an issue in the church.

These people had been hurt and bruised by the church and its view of the Bible. The Bible was used as a hammer instead of an illuminator for who God is, what he has done to change the world, and how he is working right now in our midst. It seemed like this Bible separated insiders who knew the truth from people who didn't and were therefore ignorant and demeaned. To be on the inside, one must line up, submit to the divine teaching, and confess the one true way. Those who think differently are on the outside.

These episodes, I suggest, are the remainders from years of living with the "inerrant Bible" that has moved from being a helpful defense of the Bible's authority in our lives to becoming a banner in the enemy-making machine. We have been trained to see the Bible as a book of inerrant words that speak a truth that must be defended against people who don't believe rightly. The Bible must mean what it says, word for word. And we know what it means, which means that those who disagree must be wrong. And so the antagonism catches us in its enemy-making machine. We lose the ability to discern together what this text means for us as a people. We become arrogant among others who disagree with us. We posture ourselves as over and above those outside of Christ who do not know the Bible as the inerrant truth. We become the church of us vs. them.

Even the Christians who don't believe in the Bible this way cannot escape this reality, for it has led them to look down on the fundamentalists as intellectual simpletons who need a more sophisticated, scientifically informed view of the Bible. They spend their time undermining the "inerrant Bible"—which is almost as bad as arguing on the basis of it. They too are caught up in the antagonism of this banner.

Perhaps the worst of all is that this arrogance not only separates us from those Christians who believe differently than we do about the Bible or what a particular verse means. It also trains us to treat people outside the church in the same way. We have a Bible to defend in the world instead of a Grand Drama of God to proclaim in the world. We have a Bible that we must convince people of, in terms of its scientific accuracy, before we can point to the healing presence of our God as illumined by the Bible and ask, Would you too like to know this God of Jesus Christ who has defeated sin, evil, and death?

The Bible of the enemy-making machine is not the Bible that can reveal Jesus Christ, Lord and Savior to the world. And so for the sake of our own lives in Christ, indeed for the sake of our witness, God is calling us out of the enemy-making machine. We need a practice of the Bible that moves us and our churches into the space beyond enemies, beyond the church of us vs. them. It is to this we now turn by examining a new way to imagine the belief and practice of the Bible as the divine authority for our lives in Christ Jesus.

god's grand drama

The Bible as the Space beyond Enemies

There are times in my life, especially while I'm coaching my son's hockey team at the local YMCA, that I think to myself, "I was born for this." I love the game of hockey, but a bit more reflection reveals that there is more to this than just my immediate sentiment toward this game.

I lived my elementary, middle, and early high school years in a place called Hamilton, in Ontario, Canada, a land very much immersed in the daily rituals of ice hockey. One of the unique experiences of growing up in Canada was the weekend ritual called *Hockey Night in Canada.* Every Saturday night my brother, my dad, and I would gather around the TV to watch hockey (my sisters and mother were less enthused). It would start with some pregame interviews and a few commercials, but the main attraction of the evening was the sound of Bill Hewitt's golden voice announcing the hockey game. We'd sit mesmerized as two teams squared off. I hung on every pass, shot, and goal. That is where something special started between me and the game of hockey.

They say *Hockey Night in Canada* is the longest running television show in the world. But it's more than a television show. It's also statistics, interviews, and old pictures, and in more recent years, the *Hockey Night in Canada* video montage. Each Saturday night there's a grand history of hockey being unfolded in each show. And every year, the Stanley Cup, the oldest and most storied sports trophy in the world, is the pinnacle of the season. It captures the imaginations of Canadian children everywhere who dream of playing for "the Cup." While there are hockey leagues and ice arenas of all shapes and sizes in Canada, it's here, during *Hockey Night in Canada* on Saturday nights, that Canadians are invited into the grand drama of it all. It's here where I grew to love hockey. This grand drama is why Canada, which has less than one-tenth the population of the United States, has more hockey players than any other country in the world.

Years later, living in Chicagoland, I started taking my son Max skating with me when he was three. He started playing hockey at age five. I remember how he'd get on the ice with this endless energy. He'd be both enthralled and distracted at the same time. One time, when his hockey team got to play a game on the ice at the United Center before a Blackhawks game, he couldn't take his eyes off the jumbotron long enough to actually play the game. He got caught up in seeing his own self skating on the big screen. He couldn't quite get what it meant to be a participant in the greatest game humanity has ever invented (a prejudiced opinion, I know).

But then, around that same time, Max began to watch *Hockey Night in Canada* with me. Before each telecast, they would play a video montage that reviewed some of the great moments in hockey history. It showed Bobby Orr's famous silhouette flying in front of the net after his Stanley Cup winning goal in 1970, Mario Lemieux stickhandling his way through three guys and scoring a winning goal in Pittsburgh. Always there'd be shots of various winners hoisting the Cup over their head in ecstasy. Aerosmith played in the background, "Dream on!"

All of a sudden Max started to get the game. Though I had explained endlessly the reasons why he should keep his body between the puck and the opposing player, how to cover his area of the rink defensively, and other aspects of the game, it never quite clicked. But now something was different. He saw himself in the grand drama. He began to picture himself stickhandling like Mario Lemieux. He could envision scoring the winning goal in the Stanley Cup. His intensity and drive changed. Before, he had been scattered and distracted; now he was focused. He even started going to bed at night with his hockey stick and asked for a mullet haircut like Patrick Kane (a Chicago Blackhawks star at the time).

Participating in the Drama

The Bible is nothing less than the Grand Drama of God.[1] It is all-encompassing. Its pages unfold the greatest adventure of all time: God's mission to save the world. Its Story absorbs all who walk into its path. It summons every human on the face of the earth to join with what God has done, with all he is doing, and with where he is taking the world. Its authority does not lie in some external arbiter's approval. The Bible's authority is inherent to who God is and the way he is weaving together all who will enter into this marvelous Story.

As we read, listen, and hear it proclaimed, a whole new world is opened. God's majesty is revealed. We cannot help but bow, submit to him, and understand ourselves in new ways. We are like Max after *Hockey Night in Canada*—we cannot help but play the roles we've been given with renewed intensity, drive, and purpose. Each time we mull its texts, we are pulled deeper into the Story and have less interest in fighting over its truth with others who don't believe. In the living of life with God in his drama, our lives become witnesses to his great works. There's no reason to fight, only to invite others to join in with this great thing God is doing in the world.

At the end of the first century, the early church was being persecuted. The author of Revelation did what the whole Bible does: he told the Story. He did not defend the truth of its gospel; instead, he drew a stunning word picture (under the guidance of the Holy Spirit) of where God was taking them:

> Then I saw a new heaven and a new earth; for the first heaven and the first earth had passed away, and the sea was no more. And I saw the holy city, the new Jerusalem, coming down out of heaven from God, prepared as a bride adorned for her husband. And I heard a loud voice from the throne saying,
>
>> "See, the home of God is among mortals.
>> He will dwell with them;
>> they will be his peoples,
>> and God himself will be with them;
>> he will wipe every tear from their eyes.
>> Death will be no more;
>> mourning and crying and pain will be no more,
>> for the first things have passed away."
>
> And the one who was seated on the throne said, "See, I am making all things new." (Rev. 21:1–5)

This word painting captures Christians in persecution and places them on task with a new resolve. It describes where God is taking all of humanity. Its vision pulls all of us into its orbit, though some—namely, the "cowardly, the faithless" (v. 8)—may reject it. What God began in creation, in Genesis, he brings to completion in the new creation, "a new heaven and a new earth; for the first heaven and the first earth had passed away."

Whereas the first garden of Genesis was the place of rebellion, curse, and death, God's new garden in Revelation has the river of life "flowing from the throne of God and of the Lamb down the middle of the great street of the city" (Rev. 22:1 NIV). On either side of it is the tree of life (v. 2). This new urban garden is so huge (in terms of geography) that it engulfs all empires. The murder, violence, and strife of Cain and Abel, the flood, and Babel are unwound and healed in the new Jerusalem, where all nations join hands to live in peace and reconciliation. It is a vision that compels, a revelation that is beautiful to behold.

At the center of this drama is the throne of the Lamb that was slain. In Revelation 4 and 5, the Lamb sits on the throne, and in the chapters that follow he breaks the seals one by one, patiently bringing the Story to its conclusion. This is how God will bring this vision into being. As the angels sang,

> Worthy is the Lamb that was slaughtered
> to receive power and wealth and wisdom and might
> and honor and glory and blessing! (Rev. 5:12)

God is revealed as the one in charge of the world, and yet he rules via the Lamb that sits at his right hand. And just as this Lamb of God rules, still bearing the scars of the cross, so there will be no violence, no bloodshed. Surely the consequences of the sins of the world are allowed to unwind and wreak their havoc. But in the midst of this, the Lamb slowly conquers, through his suffering, via the sword of his Word, through his healing presence in the world. It is a Story that swallows up the whole world.[2]

When seen in this way, the Bible is too big to be controlled and used as a weapon. It is a drama that can only be told, participated in, and witnessed to. As we open up the Bible to tell the Story, a space is opened beyond the making of enemies. As the story is told, it either compels you by its narration (by the Holy Spirit) or leaves you repelled (or unmoved) and walking away. But there is no arguing. It is the space beyond enemies.

Not a Fight but an Invitation

When people are looking to start a fight or win an argument, they generally don't begin by telling a story. Instead, they start an argument. To start an argument, you need one person to make an assertion and another person to make a counterassertion that tries to undermine the contentions of the original assertion. The first person responds, and on it goes in a back-and-forth volley, a contest of me vs. you to see who will win.

The Grand Drama of God, however, invites people to engage on different terms. It's a Story to be told, and it elicits questions: Are you interested? Does the God of this Story compel you? Does the Story engulf you? An openness comes forth in the telling of a good story. It is all part of what makes the space that is beyond enemies.

The Bible itself reveals that the way God works is through the way of the Lamb. Jesus Christ is raised to the right hand of the Father to reign as the Lamb that was slain on the cross (Rev. 5), and he shall rule until all has been made subject (1 Cor. 15:25). The Lamb, still bearing the marks of his suffering, comes patiently, by his presence, not by coercion, slowly making all things right. He is working to draw the whole world to himself. And so we go on to ask, Can you see him at work? Can you grasp the beauty of this vision? Can you recognize his presence? Can you submit right now to his presence?

Some (probably many) will reject him and turn toward their own ways. Rebellion, sin, and injustice release destruction in the world and in people's lives. The Bible is a sword that divides truth from untruth in searing terms. There are consequences to the choices we make in our lives. But this sword is not violent.[3] The Story invites all to enter this great drama, but Jesus will not coerce people to come in. He is love. He rules the world but does so as a Lamb that was slain.

When Jesus says, "Whoever is not with me is against me, and whoever does not gather with me scatters" (Matt. 12:30), he is carefully noting that his presence ("with me") draws people in to what God is doing in the world. But it is the way of love that all who come would come only in freedom. Those who resist the pull of his presence and eventually reject him outright are left to wander into directionless and destructive chaos. And so the very presence of Jesus forces people to decide for or against him, to be pulled in or to be cast into chaos. But Jesus himself does not come to make enemies (John 3:17).

Likewise, we who follow him follow in his same way. It is the way of the lamb among wolves. There is no coercion in his way. The Bible is the grand story we tell and offer to the world. We invite people into it. We give it as a gift to any who are willing to receive it. This is the space that opens in front of the Bible as the drama of God. It is beyond us vs. them. It is the space beyond enemies.

We Come to the Bible as Participants

As I already mentioned, back when we first began to plant Life on the Vine Church in the northwest suburbs of Chicago, I would often meet with Christians over a cup of coffee to discuss church, gospel, and cooperating together to cultivate God's kingdom. During one such meeting, I met John, who was from another church. John questioned me on what I believed about seven-day creation. Did I believe that the book of Genesis in the Bible was narrating a literal seven-day creation or a figurative seven-day creation? Was a "day" in Genesis 1–3 a literal "day" in terms of hours, or was it a figurative day that might actually be many light-years long? John was insistent. He needed to know this before joining our new church.

I remember asking John why this concerned him so much. He said it was because he could not minister and work in mission alongside someone (or a church) who did not believe in literal seven-day creation. To him, this belief was foundational to trusting anyone he'd be working in mission with. I explained that I believed in creation. I said that as I read the first three chapters of the Bible, it was inconsequential to me whether Genesis meant a literal seven-day creation or a figurative one. What mattered was that God created the heavens and the earth and all therein and that he rested on the seventh day, whichever "day" (literal or figurative) that meant. I explained how other things, like the historical-Adam question, played into this. This didn't cut it for John. He walked away from our conversation.

I have often asked myself after conversations like that, How do we tell what is important or essential to our faith in Christ? How do we discern what differences are worth "sparring over"? To me, the answer is all in the telling of the Grand Drama. Do we tell it as people in control of it or as participants in the Story? It is really only in participating in the Story that I can ask what difference it makes to my life whether God created the heavens and earth in seven literal days or in seven figurative days. For me, God as Creator was central to the story; all else flowed from there. For John, the Bible was buttressed by a particular view of science that could prove the Bible was true. John's belief about science was ultimate to him, and mine wasn't to me. His particular view of science eschewed evolution. Evolution implied certain things (and not other things) about what it meant to be human. But my view let me see God creating in multiple ways, and this did not diminish the very nature of what it meant to be a person created by God and who believed with all his heart every word of the Bible.

For me, the Bible is a drama to be lived into, a story to be told. God as Creator was essential; whether the days were literal or figurative was not. For John, the Bible was a tool to convince people of a worldview and ask for their allegiance. John's whole relationship to the world and his understanding of the way God worked, and even his perspective on evolution, hinged on this question of allegiance. It shaped John's view so much that he saw others in terms of us vs. them. Even if I agreed with John on literal seven-day creation, I suspect we would still differ on what it means to live life as a creature in creation with God as Creator. I believe we could work out such disagreements in mutual submission to (and dependence on) one another as we read the Bible together, carefully listening to each other's gifts, which include the teacher's gift among us, but not exclusively so. Disagreements and different opinions, as ordered by the Spirit, are tested, and we learn from each other in the mutuality of the Spirit. We grow in applying the text and extending the Word into new territories of our lives and of the places where we live. This is why a church that agrees with me on everything is the last church I'd want to be a part of.

I suspect that if John and I could have committed to true community together in the Spirit under the authority of the Bible, we would have found each other's views helpful in contributing to a deeper understanding of God the Creator and Lord of the world. But John wasn't up for that. He wanted to be part of a church that agreed with him already.

The Drama of God

Theologian Kevin Vanhoozer describes Scripture as the authoritative script for the "Drama of God" in history. Jesus is the center of this script and the pivotal climax of the Story. This drama has five acts: creation, Israel, Jesus, the church, and the eschaton, the end of the world as we know it. Jesus, after ruling and slowly bringing in his kingdom, will return, consummating his kingdom with the new heavens and the new earth. God is both the writer of the script (Scripture) and its main actor.[4] We are all participants. The script and its performance are both equally essential to living the Christian life.[5] We cannot really know the script apart from performing it. To separate "creation" from living life with the Creator sets us up for another argument about seven-day creation. To join together in living life with the Creator God opens a space beyond enemies where we can work out, in Christ and by the Spirit, what it means that God created the heavens and earth in seven days.

And so we come to the Bible as participants in its Story. Just as an actor or actress in a play might find their very self changed through the process of playing the role they've been given, so also we grow deeper in our understanding of God and how he works, and even of our own feelings and dispositions toward God, as we participate daily in this great Story. We experience firsthand the authority and power of the Bible over and in our lives. Written book by book, by prophets and apostles within the nation of Israel and the church, guided by the Spirit, and then read and recognized through years of testing endured by the people of Israel and the church, the Bible does its work today by pulling believers deeper into the Story, not merely as observers, but as participants in God's life and mission in the world.[6]

If there are differences between us over the Story, it is usually a matter of emphasis—we emphasize one part of the Story over another because it speaks into the situations and problematics of our context and is therefore, we believe, more essential. We can work out our differences over time, together, as we live into the great script of God and live within the Story. We live together in a community called church, navigating various situations of sin in our lives, and work to sort out why this particular emphasis is happening here and helps illumine the situation here while another emphasis is happening there and illumines the situation there.[7] Our differences are worked out over time as we read the Bible together. This is how the Bible works in the space beyond enemies.

No Need to Defend a Good Story

For years now, I have studied daily very early in the morning at the local McDonald's. One day a man named Stephen, a nonbeliever, discovered that I was a Christian and asked me forthrightly, "How can you base your life on an old book of fairy tales?" When I asked what fairy tales he was talking about, he listed some discrepancies he believed were in the Old Testament and asked, among other things, "How come there are two different creation accounts in the Old Testament [in Genesis]? And who was Abijah's mother: Maacah daughter of Abishalom [1 Kings 15:1–2] or Micaiah daughter of Uriel [2 Chron. 13:1–2]?" It was quite a well-informed critique of the Bible's historiography. He went on to ask how I could believe that the Red Sea divided and how I made sense of genocide committed by God's people.

These are all serious questions. But I never try to argue with nonbelievers about the Bible on these terms. The Bible is God's account of himself at work in the world through a people. It is not a scientific account meant to put God under the tutelage of a modern scientific microscope. The Bible's language and its historical accounts are meant to tell the ongoing Story. Many accounts are told in the terms of the ancient Near East that are horrific to the modern mind. These reveal more about what the people at that time thought of God than they do about what God was actually being a part of.[8] One must read carefully with a discerning eye because of these complexities. And when these accounts are examined as scientific documentation by extracting all data from its context and its redemptive story, they can't help but be misinterpreted. This way of reading and interpreting changes the nature of the Bible and in essence strips it of its dramatic content. The Bible is the Story of a God who always condescends to come and be with a people. When we read it this way, letting the drama of God hold its central place, the discrepancies are not really essential enough to be called discrepancies. They are simply different aspects of the same events. When we see God in this whole drama, we see a fallen humanity committing genocide in the name of God, not God himself doing it. Stephen wanted to get into a debate about the Bible; I just wanted to tell the Story. Stephen and I really could not work out these details of the Story until we were both walking within it.

The famed theologian Karl Barth once argued that the Word of God comes in three forms: (a) Jesus Christ himself, (b) the

Scriptures themselves, and (c) the proclamation of the Word of God from Scripture. For Barth, the Word of God is all "one and the same whether we understand it as revelation [i.e., in Christ, the God-man], Bible, or proclamation."[9] We cannot therefore separate the Bible from the incarnation of God in Jesus and our relationship with him and in him. The Bible is an extension of God coming into history in Christ and then extended (and made known) through the Spirit. The Bible's full authority thus cannot be known in our lives apart from also knowing God's presence with us by the Holy Spirit in submission to him through the reading and hearing of Scripture. Any attempt to distance the Bible from his presence, from who he is and what he is doing among us, separates the Bible from the very reality in which it makes sense as the Word of God. Any attempt to base its authority on some other source of judgment diminishes what it is and, by default, undermines its authority.

This is why, instead of arguing about the Bible with Stephen, I'd rather tell him about the Jesus of the Bible. I'd like to introduce Stephen to who Jesus is and what he has done, in my life and others, and then invite him in to know this God who has come to us in Christ. Only in the hearing of the gospel, by the illumination of the Spirit, via the presence of God in Christ, will Stephen know the authority and power of the whole revelation of God in Christ as revealed in Scripture. I'm sure there's no harm in talking about the details of the historical veracity of Scripture with Stephen, but we must be careful not to miss the point and get lost in arguments. In the words of Barth, "The promise of this Word is thus Immanuel, God with us."[10] A space therefore must be opened up between me and Stephen in which we read the text together. A mutuality must take place. And here we both will know the power and authority of the living Christ revealed in the Bible. Here we will work out these details. Until then, I'll listen to Stephen, but I will not defend the Bible. The Bible cannot be known in the enemy-making space.

Seeing the World Like We've Never Seen It Before

The Bible as Grand Drama unfolds a world we could not see otherwise. It describes, via history, sermons, poetry, praise, prayers,
and teachings, the world as it is under God's reign. Every word is
inspired by his Spirit. And by that same Spirit, the Bible reshapes
our imaginations, so that we can see God and the world under
his lordship. It is like a lens that helps us discern God's working
among all people, regardless of color, culture, or history. It helps
us see where we live in a different way by showing us that God
is at work in all people around us and in all circumstances. The
Bible opens up space.

As our world is shaped by the Bible, we begin to sense God's
very presence at work in the relationships we share, in neighborhood situations, with people who are totally different from us,
in conflicts in city government, in the course of sharing everyday
life with other people. The Bible is this all-encompassing drama
that pulls the world in.

When I was a youth pastor in my early twenties, I encountered a
young man named Tom who had been a participant in the church's
youth group prior to my being there. He had gone away to a state
university and had now returned for the summer. His mother approached me one Sunday and said she was worried. Tom had not
been able to get employment for the summer. He was spending all his
time sitting in their basement reading the Bible over and over again
and listening to Christian music. He was not interacting socially
with any of his old friends. She thought he must be depressed.

Tom and I talked several times that summer. The university experience had jolted him. He had gotten caught up in pornography
and was fighting with all his might the guilt and the addiction that
was taking over his life. Furthermore, much of what he had come
to believe through his upbringing, including his homeschooling,
was being challenged. The rug had been pulled out from beneath
him. He felt attacked on all sides.

Though he never said this, it was obvious he feared the world. He did not know who or what to trust. And so he took his Bible and went downstairs into the basement and hunkered down. He spent hours memorizing it, repeating long passages over and over to himself. The Bible had become a fortress for him to hide in and defend himself in. He was cloistering himself off from people. Anytime someone disagreed with him, he got defensive and went back down to the basement with his Bible for more of the same.

Although Tom went to an extreme, he illustrates the way many people use the Bible in our changing world. When they feel attacked, it's the only thing they have left to trust. It's the safe place where they can go and hide and take shelter from all the incoming challenges. All I have to do, they say, is pound the Bible into my brain, just know its every word and use it to defend myself from anyone who dares challenge my world.

But this misses so much of what the Bible is, so much of how it has been given to us by God and how we Christians are to relate to it. It was never given to us as the means to control our lives. Its authority cannot be possessed or controlled, because Jesus as Lord is the authority in, through, and behind all Scripture. Instead it opens us up to the world, to people who are not us, to places of hurt and pain, and helps us see God working.

Theologians Willie James Jennings and J. Kameron Carter have shown how, from the church's earliest days, Christians saw themselves as grafted onto the nation of Israel. This is an essential part of the Story. And so Christians saw themselves as an extension of a long history of God at work in the nitty-gritty lives of a people with an ethnicity (Hebrew) and a location (Canaan). When the gospel reached Rome, however, and then the emperor became a Christian, suddenly Christianity became the official religion of Rome. Christianity changed. Gradually, Christianity became something separate from Israel. The Story became their story, white Europeans' story. The church lost its story. Years later, European Christianity saw their Christianity as the only Christianity.

Instead of humbly extending the Story of what God was doing into new places, they imposed their white Christianity on others and excluded those who would not become like them.[11] This was a denial of the Story.

There is no exclusion in the Bible. There is no imposing or coercion. Rather, through the Bible, I become a participant in God's work in the world, which engulfs all people. Through reading it, hearing it proclaimed and its story unpacked, seeing our lives in its terms, we are caught up into this stream of humanity God is bringing together in Jesus Christ. Through the Bible I am able to see his work of reconciliation and renewal pushing into people's lives all around me. I can see sin, violence, and evil where people refuse God, exclude others, and get sucked into the world's violence. But in it all, I remain confident in his work to bring down the powers and heal the world of its violence and exclusion.

The book of Revelation describes where the world is going: "a great multitude that no one could count, from every nation, from all tribes and peoples and languages, standing before the throne and before the Lamb, robed in white, with palm branches in their hands" (Rev. 7:9). It unfurls the mission God is carrying out, from his calling the nation of Israel into being, to grafting onto it the church, from which a new heaven and a new earth shall be fashioned that will welcome "the glory and the honor of the nations" (21:2). In this great drama, us vs. them is overcome. No more racism, misogyny, patriarchy, economic oppression. This is the space we are called to live into now via the Bible, the space beyond enemies.

Jesus the Center

Ultimately, we know this Bible, its depths and authority, only through Jesus Christ. He is God come into history in the flesh. All of the Old Testament (the prophets) leads to him. All of the New Testament (the apostles) extends from him. As Catholic theologian Hans Urs von Balthasar understood, it is in the person and work of Jesus Christ that we see God, and from there we can see God everywhere in the world.[12] Balthasar named Christ the pure "form" by which God manifests himself in all creation. By knowing Christ, his presence, we can know and discern God everywhere we live life.

For Balthasar, Scripture was a part of, indeed an extension of, the concrete, living Jesus Christ and his authority and power.[13] In Jesus, Scripture is the means by which we see God at work in the world, not a means by which to defend ourselves from our enemies or an excuse to sequester ourselves in the basement. Scripture is the embodied lens of Christ himself by which we enter and see God at work in the world. All in all, then, the authority and power of God in Scripture is known only through participating in it as the ongoing drama of God.

Practicing the Bible beyond Enemies

What does all this mean for the practice of reading the Bible? First, we should not approach the Bible primarily as individuals, alone at our desks, using it to exert judgments on ourselves and others. It is the text of God's people, to be read as a part of being God's people called together. And so we must practice reading the Bible together as a community of believers, bowing to his presence, allowing the gifts of the Spirit to work among us in discerning truth in this book. We must listen to each other. We must discern the struggles. And then we must place it all within the drama that God is working in the world.

Each of us, as we read together, will submit to the teachers in our midst, to those gifted in study and in the explanation of the context and historical issues in the text. We will also listen to the pastors, the counselors, the healers, and others. With them we will ask not only what this text meant in the past but how we are to faithfully extend its truth to our situation as we sit and discern together. We will not be isolated in our own interpretation. We are engaging Scripture together to discern what God is doing among us and where he is taking us.

We will continue to read the Bible as individuals too. But our individual reading, prayer, and meditation are guided from our times of reading Scripture together. And our individual reading and learning is always submitted to the community for the greater enrichment of the body.

Neither will we read the Bible defensively. We will peacefully enter the world and all the challenges it presents and will open Scripture to discern what God is doing. We will sit around tables in our neighborhoods, trusting the Spirit of God to work through our gifts, as we mutually submit to Scripture and to one another. With the apostle John, we will test the spirits to know the one Spirit (1 John 4:1–2). And with the apostle Paul, we will let all things be done decently and in order, the gifts subject one to another (1 Cor. 14:32, 40). But most of all, we will allow Scripture to illumine where God is at work among us in the world. There's a difference between (a) pulling out the Bible to make (prove) a point and (b) using it to explain how what just happened fits into the Story. In this way, reading Scripture communally opens spaces for the fullness of his presence among us. In this space, any antagonism is thwarted as we mutually submit to one another. There is no us vs. them. It is a space beyond enemies.

A conflict was brewing at our church a few years ago over the issue of women serving alongside men as pastors. There were a few people seriously questioning whether women should be "pastors" at our church. The leaders of our church decided to open the space one more time to study the texts carefully and invite any and all who were interested to discern this issue for our church. We met for seven evenings over seven weeks. We listened to each other. As in Acts 15, we did this as a community (v. 12). As in Acts 15, we recognized what God had been doing in and through women pastors among us, and this informed how we interpreted the texts (v. 12). Every voice was heard (vv. 4, 5). Each night we read a text, and a leader gave his or her interpretations (v. 15), paying attention to what God had been doing in the life of our community (v. 8). The time came to seek a consensus. Even though not everyone could agree 100 percent, the consensus was to affirm women leaders alongside men. Even those who could not totally agree still voiced how they could totally trust where this community was going. They could submit to the authority of Scripture and the Spirit at work so visibly in this place. Truly everyone could say, as with the letter to Antioch (v. 28 NIV), "It seems good to the Holy Spirit and to us" that God has called women to lead alongside men in our church. The opening of Scripture in our church had become the space of his presence, the space beyond enemies.

The Pulpit Changes

Second, when we preach the Bible on Sunday mornings, let us do more than merely offer information to be used by people to improve their Christian lives, which they can either accept, debate, or ignore. The Bible as Grand Drama demands something more.

Instead, as preachers, let us unfold the drama that lies before us under Jesus as Lord. We announce the good news of what has been made possible in the life, death, and resurrection of Jesus Christ. Out of the Bible, we narrate the truths of God's character, the way he works. Based in Scripture, we make observations of what God has done and then ask, Can you see him at work in, among, and around you? We exposit the Bible as a new world being born by the Spirit.

The Bible, preached in this way, is "a demonstration of the Spirit and of power" in God (1 Cor. 2:4). It funds imagination for the way God is working. This opening of Scripture always invites people to enter and participate in this world God is bringing in. Will you receive his forgiveness? Will you reconcile? Will you be renewed and will you engage and will you participate in all he is doing to bring this kingdom to the whole world? Even though convicting, this preaching is never coercive. Compelled by the vision of what God is doing in the world, we invite all to participate in what he is doing, to respond to his work among us. This is not a new legalism. This is not more "things to do" out of our own strength. The invitation is always to join with God. In preaching this way, there can be no arguing over Scripture, only a receiving of the gospel anew each week.[14] Such preaching is beyond making enemies.

Each time Scripture is read, the gospel is preached, and we submit in prayer, God's presence comes among us and we are illumined by the Spirit. Scripture, practiced in this way, opens the space to be present to his fullness. And then, as we submit to the Spirit, we ask, How does this illumine what God is doing among us? There is no enmity in this space because his presence is here. It is a place of his fullness. We receive of his unending grace.

As we sit around tables, chewing on the sermon from Sunday morning, there is no picking apart the pastor's sermon. Instead we gather to process our responses to God's Word. We ask each other, What did you hear? What do you see now that you didn't see before? What did you learn about God's activity in your life, in your friends' lives? How should we respond? These kinds of conversations signal that we are living out of the abundance of what Christ would do for us if we will just obey, be faithful, and follow him. This is living in the fullness of his presence. This is the space beyond enemies.

And so the preacher does not stand above the congregation as a divider. He or she stands among the people, speaking humbly (1 Cor. 2:4), proclaiming the good news in all its abundance. The Bible does not separate us from others. It does not even separate us from the world. It resists the church of us vs. them. Instead, as we extend the Bible into the world, it draws the world into his Story. The Bible is beyond making enemies.

As We Go into the World

When we see the Bible as Grand Drama, part of what changes is the way we see our own interpretation and exegesis. Our own understandings of the truths of Scripture are now swept up in a bigger stream. It is not that the Bible becomes relative to all times and contexts. Rather, with each struggle, pain, and new situation, we glean new insights from certain truths. Different things will get emphasized over others. A distinctive to our church may indeed take shape. But we must resist that distinctive becoming a banner we hail as a weapon against someone else's group.

As part of being in a long story, some things will get elevated and accentuated along the way, while others may get lost and need to be recovered. We do not lose old truths; rather, we learn how to rephrase, translating them anew. We need both the old and the new to be faithful. In this way, with each local discernment, as we gather to read the text, the truth of Scripture is faithfully extended into new situations. The Story continues. It never ends.

And so, as we go into the world, the Bible cannot be an object to control or dissect for our own purposes. The Bible instead is a space to be opened up. It is a guide around which we learn, grow, and discern further what God is doing. It is the drama of God being lived, ever extended into new territory by what God is doing among us.

This way of seeing the Bible and practicing the Bible changes us as a people in the world. Whereas before, the "inerrant Bible" shaped us to assume we possess the truth, now we enter the world humbly listening to our neighbors, illumined by the Bible to discern what things we can learn and see about God at work in them. Whereas before, having an undue certainty about the things we believed from the Bible, we were arrogant toward people, posturing ourselves defensively when people would disagree with us, now we welcome other opinions and ask how or what this might mean for us. We are no less faithful, for we seek to extend the Scriptures

into new territory faithfully every time. But we are open to surprise in the process. Instead of "inerrant Bible," we believe in the
Bible as our one true Story of God for the whole world, infallible
in and through Jesus Christ.

This Grand Drama of God is bigger than me, my church, or
even my neighborhood. This is a Story to be told in the whole
world. This Bible therefore opens space between us and other
people who do not believe the Bible like we do. It opens space for
God's presence to be experienced, seen, and heard anew. Through
the Bible, God heals the us-vs.-them antagonisms in the world. It
moves us into this marvelous new world that God is working in
the space that is beyond making enemies.

5

have you made a decision?

Kathie Lee Gifford, famous cohost of NBC's *Today* and of *Live! with Regis and Kathie Lee* before that, has told the story of her conversion many times. She describes being at a movie theater when she was twelve, watching the Billy Graham film *The Restless Ones*, and hearing a voice speaking to her. She sensed it was God saying, "Kathie, I love you. If you'll trust me, I'll make something beautiful out of your life." After the movie, a minister invited the moviegoers to come to the front of the theater and "accept Christ." She went forward. "Standing at the front of the theater," she says, "I asked Jesus into my heart."[1] Kathie Lee made a decision.

God met her that night, she says, right where she wanted to be: at the movie theater. She so deeply wanted to be an actress and a singer. And so she tells of how God walked with her from that moment on, through a journey to Hollywood and the many ups and downs of her life. Part of her amazing testimony has to do with her close friendship with Billy Graham, who encouraged her over the years. God walked with her even through the difficult moments when she found out her husband had cheated on her. She was able to forgive, and they made it through those times. Frank, her husband, later died, and in Kathie Lee's testimony she usually includes how she is confident he is now with the Lord.

This kind of public "testimony" is a staple of evangelical Christianity in North America. With each testimony usually comes a moment of decision. From the Billy Graham Crusades of the 1950s and '60s, to the weekly altar calls in church services across the country, to the four spiritual laws that taught us how to share our faith, the defining moment is usually the making of a decision to receive Christ for forgiveness of sin and enter into a personal relationship with God. Kathie Lee's is a powerful example of that.

But does this decision actually mean anything for how we live? Surely receiving forgiveness by faith in Christ is important. But does it lead to transformation? Does this decision change anything? When I make this decision, I receive forgiveness from sins. I naturally feel better about myself. But then do I enlist God to help me make my already assumed dreams (like becoming a Hollywood movie star or singer) come true? Or does it change my dreams or the way I live those dreams? I am sure there are many examples of dramatic conversions, and I don't want to diminish the many great testimonies of change among North American Christians. But for this chapter, I want to look at whether "the decision" changes my life or merely reinforces what I'm already doing.[2] I want to ask whether this decision has become an identifier for Christians as to who is "in" instead of an initiation into a whole new way of life.

Jesus Demands a Turn

Conversion is at the core of the Christian gospel. Jesus's ministry begins with the call to convert. He preaches, "The time is fulfilled, and the kingdom of God has come near; repent, and believe in the good news" (Mark 1:15). And so Jesus announces God's reign is coming. Soon, as a result of his life, death, and resurrection, Jesus will ascend and rule the world at the right hand of the Father. A new world is being born. But one must turn (repent) and trust (believe) and enter in. All through the book of Acts, the apostles preach the gospel of what God has done in Christ. He now reigns. To enter into this world, we are invited to a conversion: to turn from sin, submit to the one who is king, and be baptized. To be baptized is to turn from the old life and enter the community of this kingdom initiated by the Spirit (Acts 2:38; Rom. 6:3–4). The gospel demands conversion.

As Christianity spread to Rome in the fourth century, millions became Christians. Baptism remained the rite of conversion. Many people were baptized. As Christianity spread throughout Europe, it became the norm that babies were baptized and that a parish community gathered to teach their children in the ways of Christian life. Through the sacraments, people became practiced in the ways of knowing Christ and his presence. The need for conversion receded into the background. Most Christians did not think about salvation in terms of making a decision. The only real decision people had to make in relation to Christ was whether to leave the church they had already been born into.

The Western church went through periods of corruption in Europe. As already discussed, during one of these periods, at the beginning of the sixteenth century, the Catholic monk Martin Luther challenged the Roman Catholic Church's abuses and its manipulation of the sacraments. He made the case that there is no need for the church to mediate and control each Christian's "account" with God for salvation. Instead, we come to God through Jesus Christ alone, through his person and work. Salvation is by faith alone, in Christ and what he has done. Surely the church, the sacraments, and the teaching of the Word sustain Christian life, but the Christian's salvation is grounded in being justified by faith in Jesus Christ alone. This set the stage for a whole new kind of conversion in the forthcoming centuries.

European Christianity traveled across the ocean. But faith grew cold in the North American colonies. And so in the eighteenth and nineteenth centuries, amid moral laxity, alcoholism, social problems, and postindustrial poverty, preachers saw the need for Christian renewal. The revival meeting was created. Somewhere between Jonathan Edwards's "Sinners in the Hands of an Angry God" sermon, George Whitefield's preaching of the "new birth," and Charles Finney's anxious bench, the altar call was invented.[3] People who had been born or raised in traditional European churches but whose faith had lapsed were called to come forward to an altar: Confess your sin. Trust in Christ. Receive forgiveness and commit to following Christ.

And so the altar call became an enduring ritual in which Christians of all kinds made a personal decision to receive forgiveness and new life in Christ. It became a new version of conversion that eventually overtook baptism for many Christians as central to what it even means to be a Christian. As a result, the Great Awakenings and other movements in the eighteenth and nineteenth centuries saw an incredible revival of Christian life around many parts of North America. It is hard to overestimate the impact revivalism and the call to conversion had in churches of the United States and Canada.[4]

Disputes over Conversion

Entering the last century, however, the pesky modernists of the 1920s and '30s (discussed in chap. 3) protested revivalist conversion. They questioned the idea that Jesus's death was a blood sacrifice offered to God that, upon reception, paid the punishment for our sins.[5] These Protestant theologians thought that requiring a "blood sacrifice" for one's forgiveness made God out to be an avenging tyrant. Instead, they saw God as love, forgiving and longing for a redeemed whole world. This loving God, they said, surely forgave people and bid people to work for his justice in the world. Pastors who followed this line of thinking came to be called "liberals," and their emphasis shifted away from personal conversion and focused instead on one's commitment to serve God's justice at work in society. This felt like an earthquake among the revivalist churches that had centered their lives on conversion and the decisions made for Christ at the altar call.

Many institutions and people rose to defend the significance of "the decision to receive Christ" against the so-called liberals. Especially important for these defenders was preserving the sacrifice of Christ on the cross as essential to forgiveness of sins. Revivalist Billy Sunday, together with the Moody Bible Institute and Charles E. Fuller's radio program *The Old Fashioned Revival Hour*, among many others, worked to preach the need for a personal decision of repentance and renewed experience of Christ's forgiveness for one's sins. As a result, the decision became a distinctive that set these evangelicals apart from the rest of Christian North America. The "fundamentalists," as they came to be known, were those who still believed that the sacrifice of Jesus on the cross was essential for the salvation of sinners.

After World War II, the emphasis on the decision for Christ intensified. Billy Graham's crusades spread around the world, emphasizing with an altar call at the end of every crusade the need to make a decision. He named his radio show *Hour of Decision* and his monthly magazine *Decision*. Bill Bright, founder of Campus Crusade for Christ, published a booklet called "The Four Spiritual Laws." At the end of its four points, it asks the reader to make a decision using the "sinner's prayer," which included a place for the reader to sign his or her name and ask for more information. It became the most used Christian pamphlet in the world. Other methods of evangelism were devised to lead people to a decision, such as Evangelism Explosion and the Romans Road. Thus, the decision to begin a personal relationship with Jesus became a marker of what an evangelical is and set them apart from, even over against, "the liberals"—mainline Protestants known primarily for liturgical Christianity and social justice.

But Does This Mean Anything?

Today, years later, many of the largest churches in North America are built on the idea that people begin their relationship with God with a decision, from whence discipleship can commence through the programs of the church. For millions of Christians like Kathie Lee Gifford, the decision is the distinguishing mark of what defines one as a Christian. But what does this decision mean in terms of real life?

Growing up in church, I can remember many a Sunday evening when the church service ended with the altar call. The preacher would say, "With every head bowed, every eye closed," and we would be given the opportunity to raise our hands to receive Christ or rededicate our lives to Christ. Then we would go forward to pray with a leader in the church. My friend Scott would respond to numerous altar calls, go up front, and either receive Christ as his Savior or rededicate his life to following Christ. Again and again he did this. Scott always seemed worried about the state of his soul and whether he would go to heaven if he died. Often, at an altar call, I too would feel the same tug. I felt unsure of my status with God, and so I would return to the altar again and again. I have since run into youth pastors and parents wondering about young people who repeatedly come forward at altar calls in revivalist-like youth services. What's going on? they ask. Why do they keep doing that?

Scott is evidence that there is an elusiveness to the traditional altar call. After coming forward and acknowledging my sin and need for God, a sort of transaction takes place. I trust in Christ and what he has done for me on the cross, I receive forgiveness, I am no longer condemned to hell, and my relationship with God is restored. But the question might fairly be asked, What actually changed? Why do I keep sinning? (Oops, I just had a very nasty thought. Now what? Perhaps I should go forward again. Did anything really happen? Where did this happen? In the law courts of heaven? Or is this all in my mind? I don't feel anything different or notice anything different about myself. Does this decision mean anything?) We need "assurance" that something happened.

In the history of the church, Martin Luther, mentioned above, wanted to make sure everyone knew you could not earn your way to salvation. Remember that he was battling the corruption in the Roman Catholic Church. So he criticized them for selling indulgences as means for the Christian to reduce the penance he or she had to do as payment for sins.[6] It played on good works being counted toward a person's righteousness. So Luther separated forgiveness of sin from works. You are forgiven first; works follow (from grace). Salvation (justification) comes by faith alone, "not of works lest any man [sic] should boast" (Eph. 2:9 KJV). Many years later, as the altar call takes place, we are told, likewise, that we cannot earn our way to heaven and should not depend on our good works for salvation. And yet we are also told this conversion should lead to a changed life.[7]

And so we experience internal dissonance. We know this decision to receive forgiveness does not require works. Yet we are left asking, Does this mean anything for how I actually live my life? What actually happened here? It is all part of the elusiveness of "the decision."

The Decision as Banner

There is no question that the decision to acknowledge sin, to repent and humble oneself before God, shapes a person so that God can work in his or her life. This kind of conversion is essential to the Christian life. When connected to one's daily life, it can lead to following Jesus into all he's doing for us, in us, and in the world.

But when the decision is extracted from the daily workings of a person's discipleship, it can become an abstract concept devoid of content. It can define me as "in" over against those other people who are "out," who have not yet made a decision. Even so, as we've already seen, what the decision actually means in real life is elusive. It is this very elusiveness that makes the decision a prime candidate to become a banner in the enemy-making machine. It can be used to divide those who have and have not made a decision, even when it ultimately means nothing in terms of actual, lived reality. It can be used to suit any given agenda.

When Donald Trump became the presumptive Republican nominee for president of the United States, there were many Christians who couldn't stomach voting for a man who engaged in "locker room talk," flaunted his massive wealth, and committed sundry cultural sins abhorrent to evangelicals. Surprisingly, soon after Trump became the presumptive nominee, James Dobson, the founder of Focus on the Family, made an announcement that he knew the person who "led Donald Trump to Christ" and that he believed that Trump "really made a commitment." In many churches, these are code phrases for saying that Trump has made a decision. Trump, in other words, had crossed the line and was one of us: a bona fide Christian. Trump's amoral life is irrelevant. As Dobson argued, "This man is a baby Christian who doesn't have a clue about how believers think, talk and act."[8] Christians, Dobson seemingly implied, could and should vote for him. Dobson's defense of Trump was an eruption of sorts for many Christians, revealing how little the decision actually means—and revealing that, indeed, the decision was important mainly as a marker to enable a political agenda that had little correlation with what it means to live as a Christian.

This, I contend, is how ideology works. Something that once meant so much in determining the shape of our Christian life gets extracted from everyday life and then comes to mean little or nothing as it becomes a banner to signify who is in and who is out of Christ's salvation club. We Christians must be careful at this point, for this is the beginning of the enemy-making machine.

I remember going to elementary school knowing that I was "saved." I had made the decision to trust Jesus for the forgiveness of my sins. In my own mind, I believed I was "in," which meant I knew where I was going when I died. Meanwhile, I was trained to suspect that everyone who had not made the decision was going to hell. Indeed, this was supposed to motivate me to share my faith. Yet somehow I felt separated from, even superior to, all those around me who had not made the decision. Occasionally I would be surprised, sometimes years later, to discover that friends I had assumed were going to hell were really saved; I just had no way to tell. Indeed, they had not known that I was "saved" and were assuming that I was going to hell.

This is the danger of the decision as banner. It cultivates an us vs. them mentality. Meanwhile, it does little work in our lives. So we cannot truthfully tell what difference it makes.

Billy Graham once said publicly on the *David Frost Show* that he believed that only 25 percent of the decisions recorded in his crusades resulted in people actually being born again.[9] *Eternity*, a prominent conservative evangelical magazine in the 1970s, reported an even lower percentage, saying that of the hundreds of thousands making decisions in evangelistic crusades put on by evangelical churches, only 3 percent could be located as participating in any kind of church a few short years later.[10] And so something that defines for many what it means to be a Christian means so little. Yet it serves to define us vs. them. It can become the basis for making enemies.

Oh Yes, This Means Something

One of the first signs that the decision has become a banner and that the enemy-making machine has kicked into high gear is the perverse enjoyment (as we called it in chap. 2) that surrounds the use of a banner. We notice, for instance, that we feel strangely gleeful over something that should make us remorseful. In the classic 1960 movie *Elmer Gantry*, adapted from the Sinclair Lewis novel, the revivalist preacher Elmer Gantry (played by Burt Lancaster) roams the plains of Kansas conducting revival meetings. He preaches hellfire and brimstone, masterfully stirring up the emotions of the crowd. "Sin, sin, sin," he would proclaim. "You're all sinners. You're all doomed to perdition. You're all goin' to the painful, stinkin', scaldin', everlastin' tortures of a fiery hell, created by God for sinners, unless, unless, unless you repent!" In a notorious scene, a teenage boy is stirred into so much despair and terror over his eternal fate that he collapses before Gantry. Surprisingly, the look on Gantry's face is one of excitement and glee. What should be a somber moment as this boy is faced with the horrors of evil and hell appears for Gantry to be a moment of perverse enjoyment.

Perhaps, one might argue, we should be happy that someone is pushed into terror because this leads to repentance and a decision to be saved in Jesus. Gantry should be joyous over this. And yet Gantry himself is a fake. He is a wayward, rebellious sinner himself, carrying on illicitly with women and drinking. And so it seems the experience is stirred up for its own sake. It doesn't really connect with real life. In the words of the tagline from the movie's poster, "Tell 'em, Gantry . . . save 'em from sin . . . lead 'em to salvation . . . tell 'em about everything—but not about your whiskey and your women!"

Perverse glee is a sign that groups are being formed, identities are being shaped over against an enemy, a person, or group of persons. It reveals that our identity has become wrapped around the ideological notion that we have been saved from hell and others have not. It is an ideological notion because the decision does not make any practical difference in our lives; it just makes us feel better in a strange way.

In early 2011, the popular evangelical pastor (at the time) Rob Bell from Mars Hill Bible Church in Grand Rapids, Michigan, put out a video promoting his new book *Love Wins*. In the video, Bell hinted at the case he was making in the book—namely, that maybe millions (even billions) are not condemned to hell just because they never accepted Christ's sacrifice for the forgiveness of their sin. In response, John Piper famously tweeted, "Farewell Rob Bell." Using a tweet, Piper was separating himself and his followers from Rob Bell and his positions on hell and the afterlife. Piper was in essence saying, "How dare you question that millions and billions are being sent to hell justly apart from being pardoned in Christ's substitutionary sacrifice by faith?" The firestorm that erupted on Facebook, Twitter, and numerous blogs in the ensuing weeks was stunning. Anger and vitriol erupted on both sides of the debate. It was evidence of just how much the decision had become an identity marker for so many Christians—and how much this identity depended on the other side going to hell. The anger and vitriol was a sign of the perverse emotion at work when this identity was threatened. And so "the decision" now not only separates us who have made the decision from those outside of Christ, but it also separates us from those Christians who don't believe in hell in the same way we do. Meanwhile our witness is compromised as the world sees our excess glee over people going to hell and looks away in disgust.

I know of an ordination council meeting in a denomination where a friend was being examined for his ordination. He was asked, "What about those who have never heard the gospel? Are they going to hell?" My friend thought about it and answered, "Maybe." This upset some on the council. They were offended, saying, "How could this pastor in training doubt that every person who has never heard the gospel of salvation in Christ is going to hell!" They asked, "What is your motivation then for mission?" And yet, I wonder why the reality of "Maybe" would be any less motivating than "For sure everyone who has not heard the gospel is going to hell!" Shouldn't any doubt that someone is lost be enough to lead us to be present and try to discern what God is doing in that person's life, and of course offer the gospel? Indeed, by giving up the posture of presumption, we are better inclined toward listening, caring, and discerning God's work in people's lives.

I remember once being in an ordination council meeting myself and hearing a person answer the same question: "What about those who have never heard?" The response was, "I don't know, but I suspect there are reasons we cannot know who is and who is not going to hell in this lifetime." A member of the examining committee, angry, stood up and said, "How dare you question this fact of the Bible. For if people can go to heaven without ever hearing the gospel, everything I spent my whole life doing as a missionary is a farce." We were all a bit astonished. No one knew what to say. Nonetheless it was clear that his eruption revealed just how much his identity was wrapped around this question of hell. His entire life, not only as a missionary but as a Christian, hinged upon others being sent to hell if indeed they had never made a decision.

Like that missionary, I do believe there is a hell. I also believe there are consequences to sin. I believe Christ is the liberator from sin, hell, and death and that apart from him we are headed for destruction and hell. But somehow, who is in and who is out is not ultimately in my control, or even for me to know. Instead, I see the decision as one way that God uses to call people to himself through the person and work of Jesus Christ. And it is a powerful one, because it is an invitation to join in with God's great salvation for the whole world. But the decision—as prescribed by American evangelical churches—is not the only way God brings people into his kingdom.

Can You Be a Christian and Be Gay?

When my grandmother withdrew from the Lutheran church in the 1930s and '40s, one of the factors was its stance on alcohol

and the effect drinking was having on her wider family. She took
her children (my mother and uncle) down the street in Chicago to
the holiness church where they did not drink. Here was a church
grappling with a social crisis of that day. They had as a church
discerned that rejecting drinking was an act of faithfulness in
Christian discipleship for that time. To make a decision, therefore, to follow Jesus was to also engage in practices of holiness as
worked out in relation to drinking alcohol (among other things).
The result was a commitment to good old-fashioned teetotalism.

Years later, many people in this same tradition know one another by who does or doesn't drink. Yet we are no longer sure how
the decision to receive Christ connects to not drinking; we just
know that it does, somehow. Growing up in this kind of church,
I often heard questions like, If we Christians start drinking alcohol, how are we any different from the world? How does being a
Christian make any difference? In a way, the presumption is that
the decision for Christ needs "teetotalism" to ensure it means
something.

This illustrates how easily we can fill in what it means to be
saved with the ways God has changed individual lives as discerned
in a particular place and time. Not drinking becomes a marker of
one who has made the decision. When the decision gets defined by
these markers, it becomes a banner, a part of the enemy-making
machine. We begin to need the markers, just as we need enemies,
in order to define for ourselves what it means to be a Christian,
who is in and who is out. To be saved means (a) you don't drink,
(b) you do not have sex before marriage, (c) you care about poor
people, and (d) you vote Republican. But in each case we are not
exactly sure why. It is all part of making enemies.

Today, one of the more popular sins that serves to define one
who has made "the decision" from one who has not is same-sex
sexual relations. Rarely has one sin been so elevated among the
many as an identity marker for who is "in" and who is "out." It
is one more way we make enemies.

Back in 2006, evangelical megachurch pastor Ted Haggard was accused of having a sexual affair with a gay man. Haggard was president of the National Association of Evangelicals and had been listed as one of the twenty most influential evangelical leaders in America by *Time* magazine in February 2005. On January 29, 2009, Haggard appeared on CNN's *Larry King Live* to promote a documentary about his story.[11] He had been relentless at preaching "the evils of homosexuality," all the while hiding his own gay proclivities. When King asked him whether this was hypocritical, Haggard replied, "Absolutely, it was." Then, without stopping, he stated the reason why he preached this message: "I have a belief system. . . . I believe the Bible is the word of God. . . . Jesus is the son of God and I believe in being born again. . . . Those things are fundamental to Christianity." It did not matter that he was acting out gay behavior or that his own decision to follow Christ did not result in abating his gay sexual behavior. He had made a decision to be a Christian, and being a Christian meant preaching against gay sex.

During the show a dramatic moment took place. One of Haggard's gay partners phoned in and called him out for saying you can be a man of God and have "a bit of fun on the side." A flustered Haggard said in resignation, "You know, Larry . . . Jesus says, 'I came for the unrighteous, not for the righteous.' . . . So as soon as I became worldwide unrighteous I knew Jesus had come for me." Here, in stunning fashion, is "the decision" that resolves everything. I am a sinner. I am forgiven. The inconsistencies between what I do and what I preach are all solved. To make a decision to receive Christ means that I am against gay sexual sin.

This, I submit, illustrates the danger of the enemy-making machine absorbing "the decision" into its machinery. When the decision becomes a banner, it essentially means nothing, yet it is filled with content in order to define who I am over against someone else. A banner needs enemies. And so today, few things identify more what it means to *not* be an evangelical Christian

than to affirm LGBTQ sexual orientations and same-sex marriage.
By that we know who is in and who is out—in other words, who
has really made the decision that means something.

In 2014 the global Christian humanitarian organization World
Vision announced a new policy that they would hire gay Christians in monogamous same-sex marriages. It set off a firestorm
of anger and hand-wringing. Millions of donations were with-
drawn from the organization. World Vision ended up reversing its
decision a few days later. Over the last decade, many evangelical
Christian leaders—blogger Rachel Held Evans with a post in
2008, evangelical megachurch pastor Rob Bell while speaking at
Grace Cathedral in San Francisco in 2013, *Sojourners* founder
Jim Wallis in a *Huffington Post* interview in 2013, blogger Jen
Hatmaker in a Facebook post in 2016, and pastor-theologian
Eugene Peterson in a phone interview with Religion News Service in 2017—have affirmed same-gender sexual relations and/or
same-sex marriage.[12] Each time, a firestorm erupted on Twitter,
Facebook, and the internet. Each time, a stunning flurry of anger,
vitriol, and hate mail was unleashed as one side took shots at
the other side. The excess emotion that surrounded each of these
public declarations signals that the ideology is being disrupted,
that the nonaffirming position toward gay sexuality is what fills
in the void that lies behind the signifier "decision," and that it
is being threatened. As a result, all who are comfortable within
their identity as "saved" are being made uncomfortable. It is all a
sign that the decision has become a banner in the enemy-making
machine.

Whether we are affirming of LGBTQ sexuality or remain committed to historic Christian understandings of sexuality or fall
somewhere in between, it does not matter. The perverse enjoyment
and the enemy making that lie behind the church's engagements
with sexuality are not opening space for God to work amid the
sexual confusion and hurt among our churches. We must be prepared to make space for these antagonisms to unwind, allow the

fears to be expressed and the anger to explode, if we truly wish to clear space for God to work among us for the redemption and healing of sexuality in our lives.

Duplicity

It is sobering to think how something so good—the decision to receive Christ as Savior—could become the source of such division and antagonism. It is disturbing to see how the decision that once invited people in humility to come before God and live into his lordship could now gather us into a space defined as us vs. them. And yet this is how ideology works. Separated from our daily lives, the decision becomes our "assurance of heaven," our ticket out of hell. It becomes a moniker, a banner by which we can mark off who are our enemies.

The decision enables us to feel better about ourselves, assured of heaven, protected from hell. Secure in this knowledge, we can become comfortable in our own lives and can protect ourselves from others who threaten our structures of morality. A decision that invited us into what God is doing for the world ends up separating us as individuals from the world for which he died.

Because the decision is ultimately not connected to the way we live our lives in discipleship, much like Ted Haggard, we end up sinning in the very ways we condemn others. We cannot help hiding our own sins by condemning the sins of others. After all, we are gathered as a people over against others out of self-protection. And we do this with anger, and even perverse enjoyment. The world looks on and sees hypocrisy. Our witness is destroyed by the duplicity of our lives.

This is why, in this time when North America has become a field of mission, we are called to discern the ways we have been shaped to be duplicitous by the enemy-making machine. Can we find ways to disrupt the enemy-making machine irenically, perhaps by sitting with people, maybe asking a question about what is

driving the emotion we see exploding in ugly ways, and then listening to the fears and angers that drive people's lives? We do not
need to rid ourselves of conversion. Rather, we need a continual
conversion, daily encounters with the presence of the risen Lord
whereby antagonisms are unwound, wounds healed, and freedom
birthed. Can we leave behind the decision of the enemy-making
machine and instead receive the conversion that in Christ opens
the space beyond enemies, that moves us beyond the church of
us vs. them, that embodies the salvation that God is bringing in
the reconciliation of all things to himself in Jesus Christ? It is to
describing this conversion that we now turn.

$$6$$

---

participating in his reign

Conversion as the Space beyond Enemies

In 1999 I stood at the front of a church, wearing a tuxedo, shaking from a bad case of nerves. A few good friends stood beside me, also wearing tuxedos, and a small crowd gathered in the sanctuary. I was trying to quiet my soul and prepare myself for what was to come. I was about to get married.

For the previous three years, Rae Ann Powell and I had been getting to know each other (what some people call "dating"). And now, I was about to confess my commitment to spend the rest of my life with the woman I loved before the people of my church and family. Rae Ann sang this incredible hymn from behind the baptismal font at the front of the sanctuary. I could barely hold my emotions together. Then she hurried to the back vestibule where she followed the processional. We met up front to stand together before the minister. The rest, as they say, is history. Several years later, it's all a blur. All I can remember is how monumental it all seemed. I was overwhelmed. "This is it," I thought. "I'm giving the rest of my life to this woman."

We had a marvelous ceremony that day, an even better reception that followed, and a wonderful honeymoon in Italy. On that honeymoon, I remember visiting St. Peter's Basilica in Rome with Rae Ann, and then proceeding to the Sistine Chapel. As I lifted my face toward the famous ceiling, my eyes scrolled from one painting to the next, taking in the history of all that God has done from creation to Israel to Jesus and now to Christ's victorious reign. I could not help but feel awe to think that we as a married couple were invited to be part of what God is doing in the world. We became small before God and yet so imbued with significance knowing that this God of history would be with us, sustaining us as we ventured into his future that lay before us. I left the Sistine Chapel with a profound sense that "we can do this!"

I was forty-three when we got married. Being single for that long, I remember how strange it was the first few weeks getting used to the idea of being married. Going about my busy day at work, I would forget that I was married. I'd hurry home, walk into the house, see this figure sitting in the living room, and be startled. I forgot that Rae Ann lived there with me. I can remember waking up in the morning and looking to my right, thinking, "Huh?" Marriage was this whole new way of living that shocked my system. It was a new way of being that I was now called to live into, even though nothing felt different in other parts of my life. I had entered a world via the Sistine Chapel. Life had changed. And now I was called to live into all the blessings, challenges, struggles, and abundance offered therein.

Contrast this experience with how someone votes in an election. When I cast my vote in a national election, I in effect register my opinion. While I believe it might have some effect on the outcome of the nation's government, for the most part, that vote has little effect on the way I live. Most citizens of the US and Canada view the vote as an expression of my views and my rights as a citizen. My vote, at least in the United States, may put me in a group (a political party) that opposes another group. It may even in effect reinforce my own thinking about the way things should be. But most of the time, it's an opportunity to register my opinions, and then I can move on.

Marriage is not the registration of my opinion. It does not pit me against another person or group of people. It is the receiving of a pronouncement: "I now pronounce you (before God and all of heaven) husband and wife." And it joins me to another person. It is not a singular decision that I make; it is a rearrangement of the world into which I embark. I in fact am leaving one world (single-person world) and entering another (married world). By submitting to this pronouncement, by accepting the call and saying yes to it, two people commence living their lives together into a new covenantal reality made possible under the lordship of Christ and his presence in their lives.

Any two people getting married do not truly know what they're getting into. In fact, experience has taught me over and over again that I actually knew very little about how to love Rae Ann well when we first got married. Marriage requires faithfulness over time because we do not know the enormity of what God has called us into. It is an adventure that takes us further into what he is doing in and among us as married people and what he is doing in the world to which we are called in his mission.

The Gospel

The gospel requires a response more akin to a marriage vow than a vote in an election. The gospel is the pronouncement of a new world being born in and through the work of God in Jesus Christ. It asks, Will you enter? Will you submit (to his reign)? Will you participate?

The gospel proclaims that Jesus Christ has died for our sins. In his death, resurrection, and ascension, God has defeated the effects of sin, evil, and even death itself. Jesus now sits at the right hand of the Father, ruling over the world and bringing in his kingdom.

In Christ, the new creation has begun. Old things are passing away. Behold, the new has begun (2 Cor. 5:17). All who respond to this good news, repent of the old ways, receive forgiveness, make Jesus their Lord, and enter into what God is doing to reconcile the whole world to himself (vv. 18–19) receive power to become the children of God (John 1:12).[1] This, in short, is the gospel.

The apostle Paul gives an outline of this gospel in 1 Corinthians 15. He starts by saying, in essence, "I'm going to remind you of what the gospel is" (v. 1) and then proceeds to give perhaps the clearest definition of the gospel in the entire Bible: Christ died, Christ was buried, Christ was raised, and Christ appeared (vv. 3–5). He narrates these happenings as the fulfillment of the promises of God to Israel (several times emphasizing "according to the Scriptures"). After an explanatory interlude, he finishes the gospel with a description of Christ's ascension to the right hand of the Father, where Christ shall reign until all things have been made subject to him. Then comes the second coming ("the end"), upon which God will be "all in all" (vv. 20–28).[2] For Paul this is the gospel.[3]

The gospel, therefore, is the complete story of Jesus's life, death, resurrection, and ascension as the fulfillment of God's promises to Israel to make the world right. His reign has begun now and is on its way to completion. This same version of the gospel is repeated in multiple sermons of the apostles in the book of Acts.[4] Indeed, this pattern is evident in the four Gospels themselves and in the words of Jesus himself.

From Pardon to Participant

Often throughout the history of Western European Christianity, Christians have put the emphasis on Christ's atoning death as the payment for our sins when defining the gospel. The gospel is about receiving God's pardoning of our sin and being declared not guilty before the courts of his judgment. This was especially true during the Catholic medieval European period. Amid the guilt of penitential Catholicism and the death rates of the black plague in the medieval world, people worried intensely about the afterlife and eternal damnation. In response, the church emphasized that we receive forgiveness, pardon from the consequences of sin, freedom from damnation after death, and a guarantee of eternal life with God. These were all existential concerns among typical Europeans. The Reformation intensified this emphasis in its battles with the Roman Church.

The gospel of the New Testament, however, puts the emphasis on the entire story of Jesus the Christ. The crescendo of the gospel climaxes on the resurrection of Christ. He is risen! He has defeated the powers of evil and sin. The fulcrum lands on "He now reigns and is bringing in his kingdom!"[5] This is where we are living now. The gospel is this: "The time is fulfilled, and the kingdom of God is at hand!" Then, always, the invitation is to "repent and believe in the gospel" (Mark 1:15 NASB).

Once we see Jesus as Lord, we are led to repent of the old ways of living, of selfishness, of pride and independence, and to fall on our knees to trust and depend on him, to live under the rule and reign of the gracious king. We give up (slowly) the ways we defend and justify ourselves and the selfish pretensions we carry. The account of the gospel in 1 Corinthians 15 (and in the Gospels, the apostolic sermons of Acts, and elsewhere) makes forgiveness an important part of the gospel (v. 3). The Reformation put the emphasis on this part of the gospel. It was the part that was most needed at that time: the grace of God and his unconditional love and forgiveness offered to all in Christ Jesus.

But forgiveness all by itself is not the gospel. Yet it is still the way God works. Guilt and violence poison the world and all who live in it. There are so many ways we hold on to pride and arrogance and keep doing the same things that are destroying our lives. We must recognize the issue of sin deeply interwoven in our lives, our complicity in it. If we would come into his presence and truly be healed, this cycle of violence must be broken. We must be loved, forgiven, pardoned, and restored by God to his presence. All of this God has accomplished in Christ, through his sacrifice and work of atonement. And so, make no mistake, forgiveness of and from sin is so important to the salvation God is doing in the world. It is inextricable from the way God works.

Yet this forgiveness makes sense only within the recognition of and surrender of myself to the rule of Christ and his presence.[6] And so when we see salvation like this, it's almost natural that the emphasis of the gospel goes from receiving a pardon from God to submitting to his lordship in a new life with God. This changes the way we see conversion. It changes the way we engage other Christians and those who do not yet know him. Proclaiming the gospel is no longer about who has the pardon and who does not. It's about seeing a new life to be lived in a new abundance.

The Personal and the Social Are One

In so-called Christianized North America, many of us assume we live in a society based on Christian principles. Back in the 1950s, there was prayer in the public schools in the mornings, the bars were closed on Sundays, and television programs depicted sexuality as reserved for marriage. Although there were injustices everywhere, the majority-Protestant populations could overlook them because these injustices did not impinge on their privileged world. These injustices affected people who were out of sight. Their problems were supposedly their own fault. We of the majority Protestant churches stayed away. The dominant church focused on the personal: each Christian's personal relationship with God. We could afford to leave the social issues to the government authorities. This is how "forgiveness" of sins took precedence over Christ's lordship in salvation. We distanced ourselves from people not like us, people who were struggling, in poverty, and in oppression. They were a threat to our comfort. They were like enemies.

Theologian James Cone tells us how this narrow view of salvation as personal forgiveness works to withdraw Christians from the injustices of the world. It enables the white Christian to believe that God is about *my* inward spirituality, the condition of *my* solitary soul before God, and *my* preparation for the next life. This gives privileged Christians permission to view the present life as one of managing sin and the world's problems as best we can. God's presence is not among the poor. The privileged can stay at a distance from the abused in the system. We can justify managing the system instead of changing it while entirely missing the fact that it is among the poor where God is working to transform the world.

Cone tells of a moment in his life when he realized the gospel has as much to do with this life as it does with the next. Jesus, he discovered, far from withdrawing us from this world, calls us into it.[7] In Cone's words, "The Christian gospel is . . . more than 'going to heaven when I die, to shout salvation as I fly.' It is also an immanent reality—a powerful liberating presence among the poor right now . . . wherever poor people struggle for justice."[8]

If the gospel is that God in Christ has defeated the powers of evil and sin such that Jesus now reigns over all things and is bringing in his kingdom, then we must agree with Cone. For no one can say that "Jesus is Lord" over *only* my personal life. That may be a good start, but to say Jesus is "Lord" is to say that he reigns over the whole world. "For he must reign until all enemies have been made subject" (1 Cor. 15:25, my translation). To say "Jesus is Lord" requires that he is Lord both over me personally and over the world. It requires participating in the bringing in of his kingdom in my own life and wherever he is working around me. The personal and the social are one.

And so the Christian life is not just one conversion. It is a series of never-ending conversions. In the words of Latin American theologian Ruth Padilla DeBorst, it is "conversion from individualism

to community, from autonomy to interdependence, from idola-
try to true worship, from grasping to receiving, from oppressive
dominion over creation to loving care of it, from indifference to
passionate, prayerful action, from Western definitions of 'development' to loving participation, from competition to collaboration,
from protagonism to service."[9] This salvation absorbs all dimensions of life into what God is doing.[10]

The invitation to the gospel then opens an amazing space in
front of it that heals the world. It is a space beyond enemies.
"Once you were . . . enemies in your minds," the apostle says. But
God has reconciled us to himself into one "body" (Col. 1:21–22
NIV). Indeed, "while we were enemies, we were reconciled to
God" (Rom. 5:10). And so we invite all enemies, whether personal
enemies or enemies to the kingdom, into this space in Christ.
God is not seeking to divide those who trust his truth from those
who don't.[11] He is not even content with each one dealing with
their own guilt before God. Instead, he draws the whole world
noncoercively to himself (John 12:32).[12] His presence has been set
loose in the world. The new world has begun. Let us not merely
be pardoned; let us participate!

Seeing Things Differently

Remember Tom (from chap. 4), who struggled with the challenges to his beliefs that he encountered at the state university?
He struggled to hold on to the salvation he had experienced as a
kid growing up in church. Like his friends, he had responded to
multiple altar calls at church, seeking certainty in response to the
question "Do you know where you're going when you die?" He
would often huddle in his parents' basement many an evening
memorizing Scripture, trying to build a mental fortress against
doubt. It was like he wanted salvation all for himself, safe and
secure. But the more he built arguments to ensure he was saved,
the less secure he felt.

One summer when Tom was in between college semesters, our senior pastor suggested that he go on a mission trip with some of the church's high schoolers to a part of the Middle East that was experiencing an overflow of refugees from the war-torn parts of that region. Through the denomination's mission board, they would be in a safety zone with reasonable security. But there was still risk, as there is with any overseas travel to places experiencing the struggles of war, poverty, and tribalism. Tom would be going as an older person to help supervise some of the relief work of the high schoolers, especially the grunt work of hauling and distributing large amounts of dry food stocks and groceries.

What Tom experienced on this trip was nothing short of a miracle in his life. He met many Middle Eastern Christians with very little security and few earthly possessions, whose lives had been threatened over and over. He met them as they gathered in the smallest of groups, ten to fifteen people. He would sit among them, listen, help serve food, clean wounds. In small groups, he'd see people praying against evil, laying hands on those who were sick. He saw miracles of healing, joy, forgiveness; he saw people sharing and praying for a new future. He saw the Spirit working so palpably he could feel his presence. As he talked with many suffering people, he never once thought about asking them, "Do you know where you're going when you die?" This question, such a common way to introduce Jesus in America, now seemed so out of place. People were experiencing forgiveness. They were also experiencing healed relationships, release from anger and vengeance. Some were just beginning their discovery of God and what he had done in Christ for them. Many did not yet know who this God was that they were encountering.

Over those two weeks in the refugee camps, Tom's eyes were opened. He began to see God at work in the world in a way he had never imagined. It seemed like he forgot all about himself and his personal struggles. He saw himself as a participant in God's work in the world. He saw his relationship with God as one of total trust in and dependence on God and on what he had done in Christ and what he was doing to draw people to himself. He gained a new confidence in what God was doing in and around his own life. And so when he arrived back home in the US, he saw the world differently. It seemed that Tom had been saved a second time. The way he engaged friends and relationships of all kinds was framed by expectation that God was at work. Even the way he experienced worship on Sunday was transformed. He no longer worked so hard to write perfect notes from the sermon. He listened and submitted when the Spirit spoke. He gave up trying to control God and instead just sat before him and worshiped him.

Tom no longer felt the need to divide the world between those who had made a decision for Christ and those who hadn't, between those who assented to a truth and those who did not. Instead, he began to see the world as a gigantic arena of God's slow, patient work of redemption. He recognized in people who had not yet known God a tug toward his presence, even though they did not yet know that God was drawing them to himself. Tom began to see every encounter with people who did not yet know Christ as a place for God to work both in him and in that person, if just a small space could be opened. Before, he might have asked, "Do you know where you're going when you die?" Now, he began reframing his questions as invitations: "Did you see what I just saw? I saw God working when you said _____. Did you see it too? Can I invite you into what God is doing to heal you through Jesus Christ?" Or, "I believe God was working when _____. What do you think? Can we pray and invite Jesus to be Lord over this?" Tom had discovered the gospel as a place beyond enemies.

The Decision Changed

Throughout and after that experience, Tom never discarded "the decision." But the decision changed. When Tom was with teenagers, I noticed he would offer invitations to participate in what

God was doing only after seeing God at work. He had to listen and be present with every person or situation long enough to discern God's presence at work. Only then could he make an observation and ask, "Did you see that too?" and then offer the invitation to participate. The decision was still needed, but somehow the dynamics had changed. The focus changed from receiving a pardon as part of a transaction with God to seeing Jesus as Lord over all things, including what's happening right now in your life. It went from "Do you want this?" to "Can you see this?" and "Are you interested?" "Can we pray and submit to Jesus as Lord over our lives and let him work?"

Tom's changed perspective did not negate the importance of forgiveness as central to the gospel and to the way God works. But rather than starting by trying to convince every nonbeliever that they were a depraved sinner, now Tom would wait for the Spirit to convict of sin, defensiveness, or the ugliness of hate and vengeance. He would make space for God to unwind the sin in the space of his presence, which in turn would open space for Tom to proclaim God's love and forgiveness. Forgiveness had become real and visceral to Tom because it was now placed within the whole gospel of what God has done in Christ instead of being isolated unto itself. His old evangelism techniques, because they led him to judge people, had caused him to make enemies, but now Tom made friends. Evangelism was a space beyond enemies.

Neither did Tom separate the gospel from the transformation of people's lives. A decision to make Jesus Lord over your life always leads into God's victories over the violence and brokenness in the world. He does this via his presence. So there can be no split between being justified and forgiven in Christ and being (constantly) changed in Christ. For we have not only been "crucified with Christ" and therefore pardoned from all sin; we now live a life in Christ through "the faithfulness of the Son of God who loved me and gave himself for me" (Gal. 2:19–20, my translation).[13]

Whereas discipleship in the past could turn to legalism and judgment and making enemies with those who disagreed, now it was the daily work of discerning Christ's presence in the challenges of everyday life. Each occasion is a moment "to be crucified with Christ" and to live more deeply in Christ. And this discipleship happens in all dimensions of life. Whenever we face injustice or evil in the places we live, at work, at city hall, or at the school board meeting, we have an opportunity to live the crucified life here too, to open space for his presence to work, announce that Jesus is Lord and working, and make space for God to transform the world.[14] It is a discipleship beyond enemies. There is no split in our discipleship between personal and social. This is how he works in our souls. This is how God works in the world.

Beyond Enemies Doesn't Mean No Enemies

Perhaps at this point you're hearing the voice of that missionary from the last chapter going off in your head. If the decision doesn't matter as a way to keep people from going to hell, then why would I be a missionary? My entire life (as a missionary) is a total waste if they were all going to heaven anyway! Is there no justice for all the sin in the world? No punishment for evildoers? Is everybody just going to be saved anyway?

The apostle Paul describes the witness of the gospel as a triumphant carnival of victory, liberation, and celebration through every town and village led by Christ. As we are led in this parade through town, "the fragrance that comes from knowing Christ" permeates the very air people breathe. "For we are the aroma of Christ to God among those who are being saved and among those who are perishing; to the one a fragrance from death to death, to the other a fragrance from life to life" (2 Cor. 2:15–16). The gospel comes like a fragrance, a nonviolent, pungent reality that one either receives with embrace or turns away from in repulsion. The aroma is zesty. It may provoke reaction. But in itself it is nonviolent. It just is. It does not make enemies, but it surely exposes enemies. It reveals what is already happening—life or death—and invites people to join in the procession.

After returning from the refugee camps, Tom saw that the missionary's way of thinking about salvation misses the point. If Jesus Christ is now ruling over all things, then peace, forgiveness, reconciliation, healing, and renewal are breaking out wherever he is recognized. It's not necessarily that people are going to hell if we don't get to them in time; rather, it's that all these people and places are missing out on the greatest possible news in this world of pain, sin, hate, evil, and violence. I must go and be present in their lives so that I can point out to them, when it is obvious, that Jesus is at work in their brokenness and that he comes to save and heal.

Of course, with great grief, we know people still go to hell. Sadly, upon hearing the good news, there will be some people who dig in, defend themselves, and double down into the destructive life of sin and death. The gospel is the means by which God unchains people locked into patterns of violence, sin, and evil. But the gospel itself is never coercive. Proclaiming the good news does not make enemies. It reveals enemies. Always offering grace and forgiveness, it opens a space that is beyond enemies.

The Space That Disrupts

When Jesus's ministry takes him through some grainfields on a Sabbath, his disciples pick some grain for their hunger. The Pharisees jump on this as a violation of Jewish law, accusing Jesus and his disciples of being unfaithful Jews. Jesus does not directly defend himself against the accusation. He asks questions. He opens space. Then he announces a new reality. "The Son of Man," he says, "is lord of the sabbath" (Matt. 12:8). As they continue on, Jesus and the disciples pass a man with a shriveled hand. The Pharisees seek to trap him again. They ask, "Is it lawful to cure on the Sabbath?"

(v. 10). Jesus again asks questions, tells a story, and heals the man. He displays the new world breaking in. The Pharisees are outraged. The masses everywhere are in awe of these great miracles, but the Pharisees see him as a threat to their established power. But Jesus doesn't participate in the enemy making. The Gospel writer describes all that is happening with a quote from Isaiah 42: "He will not quarrel or cry aloud, nor will anyone hear his voice in the streets; a bruised reed he will not break, and a smoldering wick he will not quench, until he brings justice to victory; and in his name the Gentiles will hope" (Matt. 12:19–20 ESV).

Nonetheless, his healing presence disrupts the world and can even divide it. As Jesus walks through town (still in Matt. 12), a demon-possessed man who is blind and mute is brought to him. He casts out a demon, and the people are amazed at his presence, his power, and his authority to heal and renew. The Pharisees try to paint him as Satanic for doing such things, but again Jesus doesn't argue directly with them. He asks questions. He speaks a piercing word of truth, asking: How can Satan cast out himself? He then says that "blasphemy against the Spirit" is unforgivable (v. 31 ESV). It sets you on a trajectory against God that only gets worse.

Jesus isn't making enemies by his presence. But his presence does reveal people who are the enemies of God. And this revealing can cause them to dig in even more. He summarizes it by saying, "Whoever is not with me is against me, and whoever does not gather with me scatters" (Matt. 12:30 ESV). Those who reject the fullness of Christ's presence are scattered into the world to be tossed into its antagonistic frenzy. Instead of entering into God's very presence in Christ, they become defined by what they are against. Jesus does not create enemies, but he does disrupt the enemy-making machine and, by doing so, reveals those who love being enemies.

When the disciples encounter someone casting out demons in Jesus's name in Mark's Gospel, they get defensive. How dare this person (who is one of "them," not "us") use the authority of Jesus? Jesus responds, "Do not forbid him; for no one who does a mighty work in my name will be able soon after to speak evil of me. For he that is not against us is for us" (Mark 9:39–40 RSV). In stunning fashion, Jesus makes clear that even though this person may not yet be a disciple, he is headed in our direction. This person is not part of the enemy-making machine. He is being drawn into the life of God's presence.

This is the way God is working to save the world.[15] It is not ours to separate those already "in" from those "outside," those who are "us" from those who are "them." We are to be his presence, to extend his presence and open up space for his lordship to be recognized, his forgiveness received, his kingdom made visible for the world to see. Though this space may disrupt the world and in the process reveal enemies, this space is nonetheless beyond enemies.

Our first question, therefore, is not, "Do you know you are a sinner condemned to hell?" Rather, tend to the presence of God working in someone's suffering, someone's guilt, their pain, and even in their smiles and joys, whatever their situation in life. When the time is right, we proclaim, "I believe I see God is working in you to _____. Can you see this too? Would you like to enter into the salvation he is working in and through Jesus Christ as Lord?" People are always on their way to the kingdom, unless they opt out otherwise. But that is not our call. We are witnesses only, not members of a jury, not executioners, and certainly not the judge.[16]

When We See Salvation Like This

Every Wednesday night when I'm not traveling, at approximately eight o'clock, after family dinner has finished, I walk out the door and head to Pot Belly Pub in Westmont. It's about a three-block walk. Two other guys from my church have sometimes met me there. We go to talk, to work out life's worries and troubles, but our main goal is to simply be present to the presence of God at work in the many people who come to this bar. We go to chill out, relax, and be with people.

As I arrive, the bartender sets before me a light beer (I never have more than two in one night), and I have a few peanuts. I pray the *epiclesis*, the old Catholic Eucharistic prayer in which the priest invokes the presence of the Spirit to make the presence of Jesus real in the meal. I'm inviting Jesus's presence to become real in this space. I know he is already working, but with this prayer I'm making space in my own consciousness for his presence to become visible. At our church we call this the "half-circle space" of our lives. Part of discipleship in Jesus is locating a place to be regularly committed where I can be present to what God is doing among people who are not part of our church. We especially seek to be with people in hurting, marginalized, and/or broken places.

If the gospel is that God has fulfilled his promise to Israel to make the world right in Jesus Christ, if indeed he has made him Lord and is reconciling the whole world to himself, then I must believe that this is true of Pot Belly Pub on a Wednesday night as well. When we see salvation like this, we can no longer enter Pot Belly armed with a prepackaged gospel that prejudges people as us vs. them before we have even listened to them. Instead we enter this place as an arena of the Holy Spirit where God is already working. We go to learn, grow with God, and see him at work. We go to be present to his presence so we can witness what he is doing and proclaim the good news to the suffering and hurting, those who haven't already recognized that God is drawing them to himself. Many times this includes me.

Everything changes in the way I practice evangelism. My posture becomes open to the world. We go as listeners, giving up power, to be present to his presence at work in the world. We do not have to impose or coerce. We do not have to peddle or convince. "For we are not peddlers of God's word like so many; but in Christ we speak as persons of sincerity, as persons sent from God and standing in his presence" (2 Cor. 2:17). After months of being there, episodes arise, real moments when God is moving. In response, we pray, tell stories, and sometimes open up Scripture to explain what God is doing. Together we join with people to recognize God in their lives and make that step to participate. In other words, we proclaim the gospel.[17] Inevitably there are moments of profound conversion.

We move from trying to convince people of one version of the gospel to opening ourselves to proclaim the multitude of ways the Lord is working in and through all things to heal, renew, forgive, and reconcile. We must first listen and tend to what he is doing in order to witness and invite people into the kingdom and into his lordship over their lives and circumstances.

Discipleship

Several years ago, at a church where I was not a pastor, I would meet regularly with men seeking faithfulness in their lives. We were unwinding patterns, habits, attractions, lusts, and sundry other things that were destroying our lives. There were men among us struggling with pornography, a man who cross-dressed, and another involved with prostitutes. One man, named George, was on the worship team of the church and was struggling with same-sex sexual attraction. Most of us were straight men carrying on bad sexual habits we had learned in the sick worlds of business and social life in Chicago.

What strikes me about this group many years later is the tenacity with which the members listened to one another. We were disciplined in asking questions, unwinding the things going on in people's lives, and discerning the Spirit's work before we ever offered wisdom from our lives and from the Bible and challenged one another to faithfully respond to what God was doing among us. Even though we were all committed Christians, none of us came to this group with judgment. We were seeking to find ourselves in what God was doing.

George shared that he'd been hanging out in gay bars and experimenting sexually. He needed space to unwind the journey he'd been on. In elementary school, he did not fit in. He was bullied and had many embarrassing moments in his life when he was ridiculed for his so-called femininity. His dad would scold him, offering little support in these moments. George got involved in gay pornography when he was twelve, searching for answers. He'd been sexually abused by a man he had trusted. He had a failed relationship with a woman and a son from that relationship. More than anything, George needed to know he was loved and supported, that God had created him for his purposes, and most of all, that the guilt he was feeling was covered in Christ and that he was in the true presence of God. George didn't need everything in his life to be judged. Nor did he need it all to be affirmed.

It took months for George to be comfortable talking. He was tormented by bad experiences of church in the past. He had to grow in trust. Most of us straight men, many of us in our late twenties, were facing similar questions. What role does desire have in our lives, especially some addictive desires surrounding sexuality? We had to ask ourselves how and in what ways it was appropriate to look at a person sexually. George needed weeks, indeed months, to ask these questions. Like the rest of us, he had to unwind what the role of desire would be in his life. It had become so central to understanding who he was. He had never had the space to even consider this question. He had to ask, What will I and should I teach my son about desire? Slowly, by the Spirit, his franticness calmed down. As he grew deeper in his integration, some desires were let go, some nailed to the cross, some ordered in wonderfully fruitful ways. There were things in George's gay life that we affirmed, like the longing for deep friendships with men. There were things we were all nailing to the cross, like the giving in to lust for bodies.

What is remarkable is that, because we were present with each other and with the presence of Christ among us, because we did not see ourselves as enforcers of a moral code—although we (some of us) knew the history of Christianity on sexuality, including gay sexuality—a space was opened up. God was present. And the Bible could be discerned, not primarily as a rule book, but as a great drama God had invited us into to be redeemed. The gifts of pastoral care, faith, discernment, and even prophecy were unleashed in this circle. This space never ventured once to create an us vs. them. We applied the Bible's teachings first toward issues of lust and desire, not heterosexual versus gay attraction. We did not treat George any differently than anyone else. We were all sinners. We were all sorting out our lives. It was a space beyond enemies.

One of the greatest things I remember coming from this time was my (and others') deep conviction that the way our church idolized sexual attraction between good-looking men and women as the foundation for dating and marriage was flat-out wrong and dishonoring to God. For us straight men, it commoditized women. It took months for us to deprogram from this worldly obsession. If we were prejudging George, we never would have seen this sin at work in our own church and in our own lives.

But this process also changed George. "Attraction" took on a different role, and the way it worked out just changed. He wasn't suddenly attracted to women as we straight men had been. But in the end, as we all dealt with lust of all kinds, we all had changed in that regard. The place of attraction changed for us all. Now we wanted to grow in our attractions and desires toward monogamy, and if that didn't happen, we were fine with being single. This space, in a men's group, gave George breathing room. It reshaped how all of us, whether gay, straight, or other, thought about sex, identity, and attraction. It placed all of those things within the marvelous reshaping of the world toward restoration and renewal and God's kingdom. Jesus became Lord of our sexuality in this place.

Over and over again, as we would be present to a person in the group, we sensed God working by his presence through a relationship, in a struggle, in a memory, in a piece of brokenness revealed, and we could say to one another: "I see Jesus working in this. Jesus is Lord over this. Can you trust him?" It always came as good news, opened up space for God to work, and set us on one more journey into healing and renewal.

For years, we in North America have practiced discipleship via a Bible study application model. We sit together, reading Scripture and often listening to sermons, learning what new life in Christ demands of us. We then exhort each other to live this way by the power of the Holy Spirit. Discipleship in this model is primarily a cognitive, individualistic process through which the new disciple learns from the text what is right and then is challenged to obey by the Spirit. This perhaps worked when one's bodily habits still remained formed within the matrix of the Christian ethos of a Christianized country. After the sexual revolution, however, in the midst of the secularized hedonistic and affluence-based cultures of today, we need more. We need places of presence, like that men's group, where by God's Spirit we can be transformed into his kingdom.

For this to happen, we must have social spaces where we can cultivate and tend to his presence together. We must have places where we tend to each other in the midst of the struggles of everyday life. For me, this place has been best cultivated through a regular weekly practice around table fellowship in the neighborhoods. Here we gather weekly, about ten of us, to submit to a meal, usually a potluck meal, and a Eucharistic prayer.[18] Here we sit around a table, eat, catch up on the week, listen to each other, tend to the presence of God at work in and among each one of us. A trusting place grows. We discuss life itself. It is out of everyday life that we discover what it means for Jesus to be Lord at work. We learn to be forgiven and to forgive in Jesus's name. We discuss sermons or the Sunday school lesson from that week. But it is done in relation to our concrete lives. Conflicts arise and we reconcile. Each reconciliation reveals new places to grow, confess, and move into in the future. We have a time of kingdom prayer, submitting all things to his lordship. We pray for life situations and our neighbors. This to me is true discipleship.

As We Go into the World

With this way of understanding salvation and conversion, we live with generous hearts that overflow with mercy and prayer for the world. We meet people, no matter how broken or strife-ridden, already believing God is working and his presence active. We are never coercive with the gospel. We never sit in judgment over someone. We discern with someone out of deep relationship. We ask questions. We offer observations when asked. And we live in this way because we know God is at work in all things, and we are only participants in his power when we are in submission to him.

Hypocrisy, duplicity, and antagonism plague "the decision" when it is separated from everyday life. But when we engage what God is doing to save people in the space beyond enemies, we are reminded of our own sin and limitations. We do not presume to be better than those who have yet to meet Christ. We too are on the way. We are ahead of others who do not yet know Christ only to the extent that we know the depths of our own sin. In the words of Sri Lankan pastor Daniel T. Niles, "Christianity is one beggar telling another beggar where he found bread."[19] We are all sinners saved by grace. And so we enter every place of evangelism or discipleship humbly knowing we have as much to see and learn from God in this moment as does the person and/or systems we are sitting with. This saves us from being hypocrites.

This is the way we share kingdom life in the neighborhood. This is the church beyond "us vs. them." Conversion is dialogical, always happening in these social spaces. This is the way the kingdom works. This is the way God works. The sign of the true gospel is that it opens space that is truly beyond enemies.

7

let's make america christian again?

When I was growing up, my church would put on a missionary conference every fall. The people we often refer to as "international workers" today— those who go overseas to spread the gospel to other countries—were called "missionaries" back then (and still are in some places). They would come to our church from countries across the globe to attend a week of meetings. Every night during the conference, one of the missionaries would stand before us and tell wonderful stories of people getting saved. The church even had a "missionary museum" in the basement, where artifacts from various cultures around the world were displayed. Flags from countries near and far draped the whole sanctuary. A sermon out of Matthew 24:14 reminded us that the gospel shall be preached to all nations, "and then the end will come." It all headed toward a climax on Sunday night when we would pass offering plates and take in the pledges of church people to give sacrificially to support our missionaries around the world. We would sit with great anticipation as a man up front calculated each new pledge and added it to the total. It was a great week of celebrating world mission, and it profoundly shaped how we thought about mission.

One Sunday morning in January of 1968, during regular Sunday morning worship, I remember the pastor (my dad) somberly moving to the pulpit and announcing that six missionaries had been killed in Vietnam by North Vietnamese soldiers. The congregation just sat there in shock. I vividly remember the confusion I felt that day. The Vietnam War was going on. We prayed for the families of those who had been killed and for protection of the Vietnam churches. We also prayed for the US soldiers. Yet it was a time of great protest in the United States over the war. Many were outraged over the US military fighting in Vietnam. But many in our church (even though we were in Canada) were saying that, now more than ever, the US military should stay in Vietnam. They are protecting our missionaries, they said. They are holding back evil so that our missionaries can faithfully preach the gospel!

The missionary conference and the murder of missionaries in Vietnam speak to how we thought about mission back then. The US and Canada were Christian nations. The gospel was about individual salvation and needed to be preached to individuals first. Because the US and Canada were Christian nations, we could at least assume people knew the gospel here. This meant that mission wasn't needed here but overseas. Furthermore, it was our job to make sure the government was doing the Christian thing. The Vietnam War was okay if it made mission possible and promoted democracy—which meant freedom to be a Christian in a communist country. Strangely, we were blind to the evils of the military interventions made by the US and other Western countries. That question seemed too big for us. The US was doing everyone else a favor by being in Vietnam. Or so we thought. We didn't see the colonialism, exploitation, and racial bigotry that often characterized US policy and its interventions into nations of the global South.

Today, we grimace at the colonialism of Western missions in the past. We are not so sure about governments being Christian either. Nonetheless, by and large, we still believe that Christians are supposed to make a difference in the world. If Jesus is Lord of the world, if he "must reign until he has put all his enemies under his feet" (1 Cor. 15:25), then surely we should see evil being dealt with justly wherever Christians bring the gospel. Surely, then, we should support the government doing Christian things. Right? We should also be working to bring an end to war, bigotry, and injustice. But should the church seek the help of government in bringing God's justice? Should the government do the church's work? Should the government be Christian?

Working for Justice: Should We or Shouldn't We?

For many years prior to the Civil War, Christians in North America led in the work of justice. It is true that some of the wealthier established Protestant churches and institutions supported the status quo regarding slavery and economics.[1] But many holiness and revivalist movements back then led the country in working for the abolition of slavery, the improvement of factory conditions for laborers, voting rights for women, prison reform, the humane treatment of the mentally ill, and the temperance movement.[2] Churches leading in these efforts were working for a world that embodied living under the reign of Christ. They believed that God could use America to usher in his kingdom. They saw the United States as becoming a Christian nation.[3]

After the Civil War, however, North American churches went back and forth on how to engage social injustice. In the 1920s, mainline Protestant churches pushed for God's social justice to be the center of his salvation. Conservative churches (called "fundamentalists") reacted negatively, accusing the mainline churches of diminishing the importance of personal repentance, forgiveness of sin, and hell. They feared that personal salvation in Christ and his sacrificial atonement on the cross were being lost and now said that social justice was *not* what salvation in Christ was about (this is known as the "Great Reversal" by scholars of American church history).[4]

After World War II, things changed again. This time there was an "uneasy conscience" among these same fundamentalists (now called "evangelicals") over the lack of engagement with the social justice and cultural concerns of the day.[5] Many evangelicals pushed for a more intellectually and culturally engaged faith.[6] Though they remained committed to personal salvation in Christ alone, they believed cultural and intellectual engagement was essential to witness.

This all led to the emergence of new Christian voices for engagement of social issues just a few decades later. One of the key voices was Jerry Falwell Sr., a pastor in Lynchburg, Virginia. In 1980 he gathered hundreds of pastors and several denominational leaders to form the "Moral Majority" in an attempt to force moral change in society through the church's involvement in politics. In a book titled *Listen, America!* he declared the church must work through the ballot box to "turn America around or prepare for her destruction."[7] He took up the notion that America once was and always was intended to be a Christian nation. Many other organizations followed suit, including the Christian Coalition, the Family Research Council, the Traditional Values Coalition, the American Family Association, and Focus on the Family. They organized hundreds of thousands of Christians to vote along lines believed to reclaim the Christian moral foundation of the country. The theme that emerged continuously among these groups was the fight to reclaim the United States as a Christian nation. In the words of Jerry Falwell, "We must never allow our children to forget that this is a Christian nation. We must take back what is rightfully ours."[8] Since those days, millions of Christians have been convinced to vote for candidates and work for organizations advocating the return of the United States to its roots as a Christian nation.

The Banner of "Christian Nation"

The idea of the United States becoming a Christian nation has positive roots in American church life. As historian Donald Dayton said, people working against slavery, supporting women's rights, and fighting poverty "supported the broader expectation of a Christian America."[9] But, as with anything, once a belief gets sucked into the enemy-making machine, it becomes dangerous to our health as Christians.

Before the Civil War, for many Christians there was no disjunction between personal salvation (a person being right with God) and social salvation (the transformation of society). Christians worked among the poor and hurting. They worked on the ground with individuals as well as social systems.

But the back-and-forth contentions over justice and salvation (recounted above) that took place between the Civil War and the World Wars seemed to separate personal from social salvation. This set the stage for a new kind of fight for the Christian nation. Here, the idea of a Christian nation became removed from the daily engagement of real-life injustices by Christians and became a banner around which leaders could rally one group of people over against another in order to get them to vote a certain way. Instead of working out disagreements over how to engage a social issue on the ground, face-to-face, with real people and real situations, we began to rally people who agree with us over against those who disagree, and we did this all under the banner of the Christian nation.

As Christians work to get a certain piece of legislation enacted by our local congressperson, we use the Christian-nation banner to demonize anyone who disagrees with us. Anger is stirred up. And we use that energy to gather people around our cause. Christians begin to gain their sense of identity as being pro-life, for example, by waging war against those who disagree with antiabortion legislation. We don't engage real women caught in the socioeconomic and cultural dilemmas surrounding "out-of-wedlock" births. Instead, we get sucked into an antagonism before we even know it. This is the way the enemy-making machine works.

Returning to that Sunday evening church meeting after 9/11 (mentioned in chap. 2), while my wife Rae Ann and I were preparing the room for the meeting, I noticed that the communion table had the US flag draped over it. The church that had used the building earlier that day was expressing its solidarity with the nation during the 9/11 crisis. Nonetheless, I was compelled to remove it. I was convicted that the flag, the symbol of the nation, must never trump the table, the symbol of God's people submitted to the very presence of Christ among us. Even in this most egregious of circumstances, I believed we must not confuse our allegiance to Christ with our allegiance to country.

Remember that we gathered somberly that night. We were talking through how we all felt about what had happened. I had asked how we might best pray for our country. Remember the older man who stood up, steeped in anger, and said, "I believe God has one thing for us to do: to go kick some a** and teach these people a lesson." Many nodded their heads in agreement. You could feel the surge of righteous anger in the room. Like the church that put the US flag across the altar, some people in our group declared that "God is on our side." Just as the US Congress had stood on the steps of the Capitol on 9/11, promised vengeance on whomever had done this, and then sang "God Bless America," most people in the room that night believed it was right to think of this attack as an attack against God and everything God stood for. It was an attack against our Christian nation! We are therefore justified in attacking back.

As some calm returned to the room, I quoted what pastor E. V. Hill had said earlier in the week on TBN: "Our president [George W. Bush] . . . says he wants the leader [Osama bin Laden] dead or alive. We want the leader alive and saved."[10] I challenged our group to pray for Osama bin Laden and for Muslims in our neighborhoods and around the world, that God would use this time to open up space for his gospel. Confusion filled the room. Anger was muffled. We left knowing much work remained to be done in order to love and engage our broken world for Christ.

The idea of the Christian nation took over the room that Sunday after 9/11. We were close to being sucked into the enemy-making machine of seeing all Muslims as the enemy. As opposed to being a people seriously engaging the hurt, pain, and suffering that resulted from 9/11, we were in danger of being distanced from the very people God had called us to minister to. In the name of the Christian nation, we were making enemies. This I contend is what happens when something very good at its beginning—the work for justice in our country—becomes separated from the actual lived reality of a people working out Jesus's kingdom on the ground with real people. Something good can become a banner that unites us against an enemy.

Jerry Falwell or Jim Wallis: What's the Difference?

A banner happens when an articulated belief that helps us navigate our day-to-day relationship with God becomes an abstract slogan around which we make enemies. A good sign that a belief has become a banner is that it stirs intense allegiance from people, all while no one can seem to nail down what it really means. It can mean many things to many people, and yet it still drives people to anger and rallies them for the cause. This is what makes for a good banner.

For many Christians, being a Christian nation means pro-life legislation, prayer in public schools, and pro-family legislation that includes an anti-gay-marriage amendment. In the name of the Christian nation, people argue for keeping "under God" in the Pledge of Allegiance or putting "Christ back into Christmas." Often when people question whether the US is a Christian nation,

Christians will try to prove that the founders of the United States were Christians and intended to found a Christian nation.

What is stunning about all this activity is that no one really knows how any of this would make a nation Christian. Even if we enacted all this legislation, would our nation be Christian? If a Christian is someone devoted to following Jesus, who has yielded his or her life to the Holy Spirit, who has made Jesus Lord of his or her life, who now engages all things (including the world) in his presence, how would any of these things bring about any of this kind of change among North Americans? We might impede some people from getting abortions. We might provide space for people to pray in school. We might even get monuments to the Ten Commandments installed in front of some court buildings. But would anyone be doing Christian things for Christian reasons? Would they be following Jesus or depending on the Spirit? Wouldn't this be Billy Graham's worst nightmare—a cultural Christianity with no personal commitment?

In 2005, evangelical social activist Jim Wallis wrote the book *God's Politics*. The book became a *New York Times* bestseller. In it Wallis argued for just health care and a program to alleviate the gross discrepancy between rich and poor in the United States. He argued for what he named the "Isaiah Platform": "God's vision of a good society" as found in the book of Isaiah in the Bible. Although Wallis did not use the term "Christian nation," *God's Politics* was in effect a stand-in for "Christian nation." In many ways, Wallis was working toward the same Christian nation, albeit a different version, with legislative tactics similar to those of Jerry Falwell and the Moral Majority.

And so the banner "Christian nation" can set liberal and conservative Christians alike into the motion of the enemy-making machine. Much clamoring and hand-wringing is stirred up as Christians argue endlessly for what side they should be on to get us to this so-called Christian-nation promised land. Meanwhile, if we're not careful, we get distracted from working for the issues of justice where we live. We do not engage how good health care is not available to lower-income people in our neighborhoods or towns because of "for-profit" health-care systems with hotel-like hospitals. We do not imagine how two or three Christian obstetricians could come together at a not-for-profit clinic, put in some hours on Friday afternoons, and challenge these unjust systems. Because we never actually spend timing being present to the lives of people living in these places. We're too caught up in the enemy-making machine of the Christian nation.[11]

We print voting guides to distribute to churches in hopes of rallying the troops to vote for the Christian nation. We take sides vehemently. We sit in the pews divided. Our goal is to win. It's the church of us vs. them.

Whether one is conservative, progressive, or denying it altogether, upon hearing talk of the Christian nation, people instantly become self-righteous. They believe God is on their side. They then argue to the death in the name of Jesus that it is wrong to vote this way or that way. Violence, anger, and vitriol break out.

All our energies are directed into this mess of antagonism. And the daily tasks of simply being present to the sick, of unwinding the sexual confusion of the ones around us, of tending to our brothers and sisters who are persecuted because of their country of origin, and of sharing with the poor all go ignored. When this happens, we have a sure sign we have lost touch with the actual struggles of justice in the world and with the One who makes all justice ultimately possible.

We don't have time. We're too busy fighting other Christians for the Christian nation that forever eludes our grasp. This is the church of us vs. them. It is the way of the enemy-making machine.

Enemies?

In order to galvanize people, every good banner must produce an enemy. Just as the medieval European church of the Crusades needed "the infidel" and the Third Reich of Nazi Germany needed "the Jew," so the Christian nation needs an enemy to blame for not achieving the goals of a nation that is Christian. Such a banner will take a person or group of persons, depersonalize them, and make them the scapegoat for our problems. They are the ones stealing the very thing we hold most dear, we think to ourselves. These are the people endangering our children. These persons become the flash point that ignites people's anger. It is a way to drive the anger and hold people's allegiance.

Few dispute that Donald Trump's campaign slogan—"Make America Great Again"—makes allusions to the Christian nation, the way things used to be. According to historian John Fea, one of the strongest factors that correlated with those who voted for Trump was the voter's belief in and support for the United States being a Christian nation.[12] Few dispute that large numbers of white evangelical Christians voted for Donald Trump.[13] He would often speak to this group of Christians by promising to put Christ back into Christmas or appointing a pro-life judge to the Supreme Court. It is therefore not inconsequential that this same presidential candidate, in the same rallies, would hurl attacks at Mexican immigrants, calling them "criminals, rapists, murderers," and that this galvanized his voting base to support him even more.

Could the "illegal immigrant" be the enemy that drives the enemy-making machine among Christians? Even though Christians have a history of caring for the immigrant and sheltering the refugee, even though Scripture again and again calls God's people to shelter the alien (Deut. 10:18–19, etc.) and reminds us that we are all immigrants before God (1 Chron. 29:14–15), white Christians, it appears, galvanized around candidate Trump despite his attacks on immigrants. He did this under the image of returning the nation to being the godly nation of his own promoted banner: "Make America Great Again." But was the evangelical banner of the Christian nation ultimately what lay beneath the "Make America Great Again" banner? Could this be how President Trump pulled evangelicals into the enemy-making machine that American politics has become in the churches?

President Trump promised to build a wall to protect our borders. Even though news organizations showed that the most productive citizens were indeed these immigrants, and that indeed there were statistically fewer murderers, rapists, and criminals among them, President Trump continued to scapegoat immigrants and to stir up his crowds against them. Even though the vast majority of immigrants were more churchgoing and faithful Christians than the majority-white populations currently living in the United States, Trump made them the enemy in his campaign to "Make America Great Again" and succeeded in getting many Christians to vote for him.

This is the way the enemy-making machine works. It is not rational. It plays on making an enemy. It extracts the enemy from relationship and makes them into an object around which we gather fear and loathing. Soon we identify ourselves with being for the good over against this enemy, even though in person, and as we read Scripture, it makes no sense. Indeed, we do not even know it is happening. And yet we have "othered" this person in a way that defies who we are in Jesus Christ. And we have done this, ironically, with the aim of working for a Christian nation. It is completely and totally irrational. But again, this is all a sure sign the enemy-making machine is running at full throttle.

A Perverse Enjoyment

Whenever someone elicits a burst of emotional glee at the misfortune of another, we should remember to pay close attention. It is a sign that the enemy-making machine is doing its work. When groups of people act in concert with such glee, we should pay close attention. If it gets irrational, be assured, the enemy-making machine is operating at full force. It does its work by tying one's identity to the banner and whatever or whomever it is against.[14]

And this kind of investment of my very self in the demise of those who are against me leads to irrational exuberance.

One enemy that often arises within the Christian-nation banner is the gay or lesbian person. For many, gay marriage and gay sexuality are a threat to the family values that undergird the Christian nation.

In 2015, the Indiana state legislature passed a religious freedom law.[15] Playing on fears that Christian businesses would have to offer services to gay weddings and other practices endorsing LGBTQ sexuality, legislatures in many conservative states passed bills allowing businesses to legally defend their right to not offer services if their religious conscience was offended. The conservative group Focus on the Family lobbied for such religious freedom bills. In Indiana, the conservative Christian lobbying group Advance America advocated for the bill because, it said, "Christian bakers, florists and photographers should not be punished for refusing to participate in a homosexual marriage."[16] The American Family Association and the Indiana Family Institute, as well as a large group of Catholic nuns and evangelical pastors, were invited to the Indiana governor's office for the ceremonial signing of the bill. Few doubted that the bill was conceived to allow businesses to refuse to offer services to LGBTQ folk in the name of religious freedom. It was a symbol for Indiana Christians of restoring their state to a Christian America.

The signing of this bill set off a media firestorm. In the midst of the controversy, an Indianapolis television newsperson interviewed the owner of a small local pizzeria named Memories Pizzeria. She asked the owner whether she would cater a gay wedding. The owner reluctantly admitted that the pizzeria would not cater a gay wedding if they were asked. In a matter of hours, the pizzeria's Yelp review site lit up with degrading insults and dehumanizing slurs. On their Facebook page, lewd pictures of naked men appeared, along with threats to rob and burn down the restaurant. In a matter of twenty-four hours, this little pizzeria became the center of a monstrous flurry of hate. Within days the Family Research Council responded and launched a website titled "Free to Believe" that listed stories of business owners, including Memories Pizzeria, who had in some way resisted offering gay and lesbian people their services. Just a few days later, the pizza parlor announced it was on the verge of shutting down because of the hate being hurled its way. A GoFundMe page was started, and over 29,000 people donated close to a million dollars in less than a week—more money than the pizza place had generated in revenue throughout its entire existence! How does one little pizza parlor become the eye of such a furious hurricane?[17]

Notable in all this is that no gay or lesbian couple actually ordered pizzas for their wedding. In fact, it is rare that any couple—LGBTQ or straight—ever thinks of take-out pizza as the preferred meal for a wedding reception. And so the pizza parlor had become an absurd and empty symbol toward which could be aimed the hate and vitriol and also the perverse enjoyment of winning a battle for the sake of the Christian nation. The taking down of a little pizza joint in the name of equal rights for gays, or the supporting of its survival at any cost, had become such a source of enjoyment, it did not matter whether such activity in fact had any real impact on the cause of gay rights. It became the place for people to hurl their anger at, from one direction or another. Meanwhile, did anyone ever get to the actual discerning of whether Christians should provide pizza or other services to gay weddings? Did churches actually talk or discuss among themselves how they should engage, or not engage, gay and lesbian people who were thinking through what it might mean to be married or not married? Perhaps, but more likely, people on both sides walked away having made their point and thus feeling some self-gratifying enjoyment over either almost closing down the pizza joint or knowing they had helped it make more money in one week than in its entire history.

This is the way the enemy-making machine works. It sets people against one another. It plays on each side's taste for vengeance and glee while accomplishing nothing on the ground. It distracts us from being present to what God is actually doing in the lives of people and the social structures that impact them.

Likewise, each time the church of Jesus Christ becomes a little pizza parlor, it too ends up spinning into the enemy-making machine. Each time we play into the sick glee of winning an argument, we lose the space for the presence of Jesus Christ to work in our lives. Amid the firestorms of anger, it is not safe for those who are weak, vulnerable, or struggling in any number of ways to come and be present and work through the struggles and pains of life. Through the anger and the violence, we lose the space by which Christ can be present and work (he cannot be truly present amid violence). For these reasons, the church must avoid becoming the pizza parlor (if we continue with this metaphor). The church must make space for Christ's presence in the midst of strife, for reconciliation, for table fellowship, and for being with the least of these—the space beyond enemies.

A Detached People Lacking Compassion for the Poor

It is strange to think how we got to this place. For years, Christians have engaged their towns and villages, been present in the halls of government advocating for the weak, led movements on the ground giving voice to the enslaved, marginalized, and oppressed.[18] They were driven by a love of people, a passion for the lost and struggling, an empathic sense of "with-ness" alongside those who suffered. They believed in on-the-ground communal activity that could lead a nation and its way of living to come under the rule of Jesus and be transformed.

And yet, over time, with the rise to power, Christian leaders gave in to the temptation to take up the banner of the Christian nation and to pursue causes rather than space for God to work. The causes could be as seemingly different as antiabortion legislation for the right and universal health care for the left. In the process, we extracted the work for "God's justice" from everyday relationships and allowed it to become embroiled in antagonism. Instead of discerning the issues together locally, we made enemies of each other. We got perverse enjoyment from winning political battles, whatever the cost. We stopped prioritizing the local work of discerning the Spirit on the ground among the hurting and the oppressed. The enemy-making machine was at work, making us the church of us vs. them.

No longer spending time with and among the hurting, we've become a dispassionate people distanced from the hurting. We stand self-righteously with arms folded, looking down on our adversaries and looking past the poor. Caught up in antagonisms of our own making, made impotent, we are no longer capable of participating in God's great work to change the world. As a result, we have lost our witness to the in-breaking kingdom that God is bringing to this world.

If we are ever to regain our witness, we must move to that space beyond enemies. We must return to being with the poor, making space to be with those we differ from, pursuing reconciliation. We must refuse to abstract conflicts and disagreements and must instead listen to each other across tables. We must allow space for mutual submission to the very presence of Christ in our midst. We must have a new practice of engaging the world for God's justice, a new practice of being the church in the world beyond enemies. It is to this practice that we now turn our attention.

8

the local church is my politics

Church as the Space beyond Enemies

Following his inauguration, President Trump signed a series of executive orders on immigration. Among many things, he temporarily suspended the US Refugee Admissions Program, enhanced border security, expanded who could be deported, and stopped the issuance of visas to people from certain predominantly Muslim countries. Whether you agreed with his policy goals or not, his executive orders and the resulting news coverage scared a lot of immigrants living in our town. An immigrant man came to someone in our church expressing fear for friends who might be deported. Our church, Peace of Christ Community Church in Westmont, Illinois, was moved to pray, to listen to immigrants around us, and to hear from the world relief organizations in our area in order to discern how we should minister among those affected in our neighborhood.

As a result, our church helped support refugees. We displayed signs we had gotten from World Relief saying "We Are Not Afraid" in our front yards in support of threatened immigrants in our town. We put one of these signs in front of the building where we gathered on Sundays. We provided volunteers to World Relief's refugee aid in our town. But what most interested me was that some of us talked about becoming a "sanctuary church."

Church as Sanctuary

The idea of a sanctuary church goes back to medieval Europe. The law at that time recognized the church building and the land around it as set apart, sacred, and so the laws of the state (or the princes) could be suspended on this property. This property would be exempt from government taxation. Whenever the state's law was deemed against God's will, it could legally be ignored or even resisted here on this land. The rule of Jesus as Lord superseded all other earthly rule in this place. Here we acknowledge we are citizens of God's kingdom first. A sanctuary church is a check on any unjust laws of a nation.

In the 1980s, a sanctuary church movement arose in the United States. There were many Central American refugees flowing into the US due to civil war and violence in their home countries, often perpetrated by the government. Yet because of military alliances, the US government did not recognize them as legitimate refugees. Sanctuary churches were those that discerned this to be going against the rule of God. So, as a people under his reign, these churches sought to provide safety and security to these refugees and immigrants in danger of being deported back to a sure death in their country of origin. In becoming sanctuary churches, they made space to stand peaceably with refugees and protect them from injustice.

In the Old Testament, God regularly commanded his people to set aside places of refuge for the protection of the accused and persecuted of other lands. He commanded Israel to treat the strangers who sojourned among them as if they were not strangers but natives. He commanded them to love each one as one of their own (Lev. 19:34). This is carried on later by the church of Jesus

Christ (for example, Heb. 13:2). Today, because our allegiance is to the reign of Christ over all other allegiances to earthly rulers, we also welcome and care for the refugees among us.[1] Could God be calling Peace of Christ to be a sanctuary church?

At Peace of Christ this idea of sanctuary church disrupted the ways we thought about politics. Suddenly, we no longer saw the voting booth as the only way to affect society. Our default first step would not be to appeal to city hall or state government. Here, right here, among us, in this neighborhood, we can make space for God's justice, forgiveness, and protection. God's new justice could now take shape for the refugee caught in the middle of the violence and vengeance of another land. The local church would be our politics.

Looking ahead, we could see that whenever we faced injustice in our town, the sanctuary church notion would force us to sort out who we are as God's people and how we should respond. Here, right here, among ourselves, we knew, we will sort out how to engage these issues in our own lives. Politics becomes a matter of incarnational social engagement. Only after discerning what God was doing among us would we go be present before the city government, telling our stories, proposing solutions or legislation for the town as a whole. Indeed, we might just discover how many people in city hall were already with us because of what they had seen of our church at work in the neighborhood.

As it turned out, because we did not own our building, we could not declare ourselves a sanctuary church. Yet the idea of sanctuary church still captures my imagination as we continue to discern the issues of our day. Discerning God's justice together, one issue at a time, as it pertains to real issues in our neighborhood, thwarts the enemy-making machine that would divide our church into positions at a voting booth. The church is a space among us that is beyond enemies, because we discern together what God is doing to heal the world and what he is calling us to do right here where we live.

All of this reminds me that there is more than one way to be "political."

The Church Is Political

The church is political. But it's *not* political in the sense of Republican or Democrat (or liberal or conservative, or NDP in Canada). It may end up supporting a candidate from the Republican, Democratic, or other party. But the church is political before any of that could ever happen. It is the people of God living under the rule of a president, but this president is Jesus Christ the Lord. To the extent that a church regularly discerns how to live socially, economically, and morally, together under his authority, by definition it is a politics. This is why I say the local church is my politics.

But it is not just my politics. It is not even just the politics of the people who are part of my church. To say Jesus is *Lord* is to say he rules over the whole world. His politics is the world's politics too; they just don't know it yet.

The dominant word used to describe the church gathered in the New Testament is the Greek word *ekklesia*, which in English means "assembly." It is used twenty-three times in Acts to describe the emerging groups of people gathering to worship Jesus in the first decades after Christ's resurrection. The apostle Paul uses the word forty-nine times to address local churches. He writes to the *ekklesia* of God at Corinth (1 Cor 1:2; 2 Cor. 1:1), to the *ekklesiais* (plural) at Galatia (Gal. 1:2), to the *ekklesia* of the Thessalonians (1 Thess. 1:1; 2 Thess. 1:1). The book of Revelation addresses the seven *ekklesiais* in seven specific cities. Over and over again, the gathered community of Jesus is labeled by this word in the New Testament.

In the Greco-Roman culture of the times, this word *ekklesia* was used to describe the legal assembly of those who possessed the rights of citizenship in a given town.[2] They would meet to discuss, decide, and legislate matters of local civic importance. These assemblies were in some ways similar to a local or state legislative body in the United States. And so, by calling the gathering of the local church *ekklesia*, the New Testament writers were giving a nod to the reality that these were assemblies discerning how to live together under the rule of a different political authority, the authority of Jesus as Lord.[3] And it wasn't just deciding matters for themselves; they assumed their decisions would impact the towns, cities, and villages in which they lived. They were describing the church as a particular kind of assembly practicing a particular kind of politics, each in a very specific locale.

Very quickly, however, we recognize that though these churches assumed they were discerning issues for the whole city, much like their Greco-Roman counterparts, their decisions would not be enforced upon people in the same way. Not all people are living under (submitting to) Jesus's rule. Jesus does rule over the whole world, but he rules through his presence becoming manifest through the witness of the church. This changes the nature of how the assembly does politics. Because this Lord does not rule by violence or coercion as the world does (Mark 10:42–45), he chooses to bring in his reign slowly, over the whole world, through witness.

Fourth-century church father Augustine called this way of politics the "heavenly city." He said the church is the heavenly city on "a pilgrimage in this world." It's a city in motion, calling "out citizens from all nations," collecting "a society of aliens, speaking all languages" into the worship and reign of God.[4] It's a city ruled by God's love, his presence. All things are being ordered toward God. The earthly world, on the other hand, is governed by violence and self-love. And so the heavenly city finds itself living among the earthly city, doing the best it can to cooperate with and support the earthly city and its provisional peace. But ultimately it does not look to the politics of this earthly city to fulfill the work of God's justice. The earthly city, you see, is passing away. The heavenly city shall endure forever.

And so, following Augustine, Christians cannot give our ultimate loyalty to a political body outside the church. Our political allegiance is to Christ alone. His reign must take shape first among us as a politic among Christians. We must live his kingdom as a political possibility first. Then, and only then, can we discern the provisional political choices presented to us by our nation-state. Only then can we challenge and resist the world's injustice and power structures as presented to us by the nation-state. Otherwise we might get sucked into the enemy-making machine. We might start to believe we can fight for justice through a nation-state called America with no help needed from Jesus. We might end up fighting for the "Christian nation" without the Christ that makes it Christian.

Doing politics as a Christian, therefore, requires that we come together locally as an *ekklesia* in each town, village, or neighborhood. Together we discern the issues we are facing day to day. With each new situation we face, we join hands and submit to his reign, his presence, his lordship, and his Spirit, and we discern how we are to respond. Our church will first be a space that demonstrates God's justice in space and time. We then will go and propose it to the world. This kind of politics will bring us together rather than dividing us along party lines. Instead of national elections, the local church will be our politics. And as we discern each issue for our community, we also do so for the sake of our neighborhoods. This kind of politics is beyond making enemies.

"A Demonstration Plot of the Kingdom"

Clarence Jordan grew up in a small town in Georgia in the Jim Crow South.[5] In 1942, after earning a master's degree and a doctorate at Southern Baptist Seminary in Louisville, Kentucky, he and his wife moved back to Georgia. There, with friends Martin and Mable England, they bought 440 acres of farmland and established a working farm community called Koinonia Farm. In a township deeply divided by racism and segregation laws, where many black families lived in abject poverty farming land as share-croppers, Jordan started by gathering people, black and white together, to discern life in the kingdom. They began by eating at each other's tables, sharing farming tips, sharing farm equipment, and having seminars on fertilizer and soil conservation. Jordan's goal was simply to live the gospel as a people.

Instead of starting with the legislatures of his township and state, Jordan decided to start a church. Instead of trying to change the laws, he started with real life. In the words of Martin England, "[If] the barriers that divide man, and cause wars, race conflict, economic competition, class struggle, labor disputes, are ever to be broken down, they must be broken down in small groups of people living side by side."[6] A small community formed of black and white people started doing life together. They practiced racial reconciliation regularly. The fellowship was deep, rich, and amazing. Koinonia Farm's mere presence challenged the ways of white people who looked at black people as inferior to them.

In the ensuing years, Koinonia Farm's buildings would be bombed, shot at, and burned merely because they existed. It would be investigated by the FBI for subversive and un-American activities. Its insurance coverage would be revoked. Koinonians would be attacked and beaten on the streets of local towns, shunned at local businesses. Their children would be ridiculed at the local schools. The governor of Georgia would sign a bill investigating the farm as a threat to "our whole stand on segregation." It's hard to believe such a small group of people could threaten so many merely by living a peaceable life.

Meanwhile, others took note, including the founders of the Student Nonviolent Coordinating Committee (SNCC) and Dorothy Day of the Catholic Worker Movement. A few years later, like-minded communities were being organized all over the South. The SNCC communities of prayer and fellowship, along with their quiet resistance, were the basis for what later became the civil rights movement led by Martin Luther King Jr. The SNCC was also the inspiration for the Montgomery bus boycott and the Selma march that galvanized the civil rights movement.

Around this same time, God was working in a black man named John Perkins in Mississippi. He and his family had once fled Mississippi because of the racial oppression and violence perpetrated against them. Called by God, however, they moved back in the 1960s and began working locally for the gospel via a Bible study, a day care center, and racial justice efforts. In 1970, John himself was brutally beaten by police officers in Brandon, Mississippi, for his leadership in the civil rights movement there. It was out of seeing the entrenched hatred of white Christians for black people that he realized the work of healing the hate in his homeland had to go deeper than civil rights legislation. Reconciliation and forgiveness in Christ had to take root in a new way of life together. In living life together, John believed, black and white persons would see each other anew, forgiving and reconciling and renewing life together. The strongholds of racism would be shaken. A new world was being born.

From these early beginnings came John Perkins's famous "three R's" as the basis for incarnating the gospel: relocation, redistribution, and reconciliation.[7] They were principles to be worked out on the ground to produce a local group of people that incarnated the gospel. Many years later, the three R's spawned a movement called Christian Community Development. The Christian Community Development Association (CCDA) has since trained hundreds of church leaders to lead and shape communities of different shapes and sizes according to these three R's.[8] The impact of these communities cannot yet be measured. But in the words of Charles Marsh, a biographer of Perkins, "Perkins's three R's add up to a social agenda more radical than any advanced by the civil rights movement, placing greater demands on white financial resources and moral reserves than even the most ambitious policies circulated in the halcyon days of the Great Society."[9]

The church communities of John Perkins and Clarence Jordan are examples of the local church as politics. By their presence they engaged the world's injustice. It is hard to imagine any church more disruptive to the culture's entrenched evils than the churches of these two men. And yet they never raised a hand in violence, even when the world's worst anger and vitriol was unleashed upon them. The churches of Perkins and Jordan are spaces beyond enemies.

Much of Jordan's and Perkins's work helped spawn the civil rights movement. Federal legislation would come that changed the Jim Crow South in many ways. But this happened after the disruption and revealing of the evil in the social power structures and systems by these local church-like bodies. As each group tangibly showed the kingdom under one Lord, they showed what was possible, and then they went to the government to push for reform and justice for others. The way God works to change the world is to *first* inhabit a people with his justice, showing the world what it looks like, and *then* engage the world, challenge the world, and invite them to do the same.[10]

In Jesus's words, the church is "a city built on a hill" that cannot be hidden (Matt. 5:14). It is a politics whose light shows forth the glory of the Father amid the darkness (vv. 15–16). In the words of Clarence Jordan, it is a "demonstration plot of the Kingdom."[11] Its mere existence disrupts and subverts the surrounding culture's evils of injustice. And yet, even when enemies are angered by its mere presence, the church never makes enemies. It only reveals them so they too can become friends to the work of God's justice for the world.

Ahead of the World

Oscar Cullmann, a famous New Testament scholar who taught in France after World War II, likened the current time we live in to that of Europe at the end of World War II. On D-Day—the invasion of Normandy, which took place on June 6, 1944—decisive battles were won that basically ensured the Allied victory over Hitler. And yet the victory over Hitler was not finalized until V-Day (sometimes referred to as V-E Day, signaling victory in Europe), after the fall of Berlin, when the act of surrender was signed by the Allied powers and Germany, almost a year after D-Day.[12] During this time there were pockets of civilians in liberated Europe who started living as if the war had ended. They no longer feared the occupying Nazi soldiers. The Nazis had lost their power and indeed were retreating. On the other hand, others could not believe the Nazis were defeated. Indeed, even with Allied soldiers patrolling their neighborhoods, ensuring their safety, they still hid food rations and walked around town wary of Nazi soldiers, living in fear. The evil forces of Nazism had been defeated, but they still lived largely as if nothing had happened.

Many German Nazi soldiers and sympathizers surrendered to the Allied soldiers as they swept through country after country. Yet there were many who refused to give up. Their allegiance to the evils of Nazism had taken over their whole lives. They became terrorists in towns and villages. They could not believe Hitler had lost. And so, even though a new regime was in charge, it took several months (even after V-Day) to bring freedom and order to some of the freed peoples of Europe. Europe had been freed. A new regime was in power. Yet many were not living in this new reality. Oscar Cullmann likened the current time Christians live in, between Jesus's victory at the resurrection and his second coming, as similar to this time between D-Day and V-Day. There's a new rule in place in Christ over the whole world. But its full realization is yet to take place.

Cullmann's comparison makes sense when viewed in light of 1 Corinthians 15:25. The verse is the crescendo of Paul's description of the gospel in 1 Corinthians 15: "For he must reign until he has put all his enemies under his feet" (NIV). It strikingly claims that Jesus is reigning already (for he must reign *until*) but acknowledges that there are enemies (and systems) not yet living under his reign. His final victory is assured, yet he goes about implementing it patiently. Through his presence, not through violence, he is reigning. Slowly, Jesus is bringing all things under his reign. Many, frankly, can just ignore his reign. They are living after D-Day, not knowing (or ignoring) this victory has happened. Others, however, have entered in and are experiencing his reign already ahead of its full completion on V-Day. These people are the church. All of this profoundly shapes the way the church engages the world (and politics).

Remember Tom, in chapter 6, who went on a mission trip to refugee camps in the Middle East? In the camps, he saw people making Jesus Lord over their lives in some of the most difficult circumstances. And the kingdom was becoming visible in their lives and circumstances. He was seeing it in their faces, in healed bodies, in restored relationships that had been broken by war and hate, in the way people shared food and clothing. People were in essence entering the world under Jesus's reign by submitting their lives, circumstances, and the world around them to the lordship of Christ.

As a result, Tom no longer saw salvation as merely a personal decision in which I get something from God if I indeed do something in relation to him. He now saw it as entering into this new social world being born wherever people make Jesus Lord of their lives and their circumstances. Salvation is not an ultimatum: Do this or else. It is an offer: Look, see the new world being born in Christ Jesus! Behold, sin, evil, and even death have been overcome. Are you interested? Won't you enter in?

The world is heading toward the final culmination of Jesus's reign, when every knee shall bow, and the whole world shall recognize him as Lord. But the world "ain't there yet." All around us are those who do not yet recognize what is happening. They are still afraid. They run on me vs. you, us vs. them. Like the people still living in fear in Nazi Germany, not yet knowing there was a new ruler in charge of the world, they are defending themselves, operating as if violence is the only game in town. They must first see another way, open themselves to his presence, encounter the reality of the way God works, see the kingdom in all its power. I cannot expect them to live like Christians if they have not yet become Christians. This shapes the way the church engages the world and its politics.

All this means that the difference between Christians and the world is not a spatial one; it's an eschatological one. It's not an us-vs.-them difference. It's a matter of timing. There are not two spaces: the space of the ones who are "in" and the ones who are "out." Rather, the church is already where the world is heading; the world just doesn't know it yet.[13] We are living in the kingdom ahead of time. We are the first fruits of a harvest that shall be fully gathered in the future.[14] We are against no one. Despite appearances, the world is not our enemy. We are just ahead of them. This church is the space beyond enemies, the church beyond us vs. them.

On Being a Father to a Teenager

I'm the father of a thirteen-year-old boy. Every once in a while, at the end of the day, I wander up to his room, have a seat by his bed, and ask him if I can join him in a closing prayer for the day. This used to be routine when he was a toddler, but as he grew older, he needed his alone time. So I make it a point to ask, "Am I welcome?" When he gives me the "OK," I love to sit with him and talk about his day. Sometimes I find myself telling him, "Max, I just want you to know you can talk to me about anything. There isn't much I haven't been through. Everything you're going through, I've been there." Max, trying to be funny, will say sometimes, "What? Dad? You mean *you* were actually thirteen once?" I just smile, nod, and acknowledge the good humor.

In a way though, it is true. I'm no smarter or dumber than Max. I'm just ahead of him. And so, like most parents in moments of discipline, I never see myself working against my child, trying to get him to do my will. Rather, I just see myself ahead of him, trying to help him find his way. I am certain he doesn't always see it that way, but I've walked the paths of struggling to find myself as a person in the world. I know and understand some things he can't possibly understand at his stage of life. He doesn't even have an imagination for the way his life will look on the other side of big decisions. He does not yet understand why things work a certain way, or what things can be if he just focuses his life and walks faithfully with God in certain ways. Though Max may not always feel it, I'm not against him; I'm just ahead of him.

It's not a perfect analogy, but in similar ways, the church is not against the world; it is just ahead of it. To the extent that the church submits to Jesus as Lord and lives in that space, it is living already where the whole world is heading, without the world knowing it yet. Like a father to a son, the church can witness to the new reality that has begun in Christ and that lies ahead. But the minute we get presumptuous, or we get into an argument, we have defeated our witness. The minute we try to control people around us, we lose. Jesus is already Lord. There's just no reason to do that! There's no reason to make enemies.

Sometimes Christians are tempted to be self-righteous. We are tempted to think the world outside the church is stupid, rebellious, and "doesn't get it!" But like a father to a son, sitting at the son's bedside, we must reject this posture. We have been blessed to receive from God in Christ. So we sit patiently with our neighbors, with the hurting, trusting God is working by his Spirit in them as much as in us, opening a conversation. And we trust that he will speak when there is space, when we are ready.

When we see something in our friends or our neighborhoods that suggests God is working, we point to it and give witness. Usually I say something like, "I believe that's God working here in _____" or "I've come to recognize God often works like this." I might read a text from the Bible and then ask, "Do you see this too?" But I never coerce or impose. I invite. And as so often happens, I end up learning more about God and his work in my own life through the person that I am saying this to. This learning posture is what I hope to have with my son as I sit next to him in his room. This is the posture of Christ's body in the world. This is the space beyond enemies, beyond the church of us vs. them.

On Telling the World Where to Go

As a dad who's working on picking up the learning posture, I sometimes get tempted to present myself to my son as if I know it all. "Don't ask questions, son. Just do what I say. I'm in charge. I know better. As long as you live in my house, you will do things my way." But how many of us know this rarely works? And it is not the way of God in the world. My job as a dad is to make space for God to work by the Spirit in this space I have with my son. Ask questions. Listen. Make observations. And tell stories, especially the Story (from the Scriptures) about how God works. When the time is right, even at my son's bedside, I must be prepared to tell him the good news that Jesus is Lord and is working in both our lives. This posture of patience is the posture of the church in the world.

Just because we are ahead of the world does not mean the church gets to tell the world where to go. Jesus says, "All power is given unto me in heaven and in earth" (Matt. 28:18 KJV). Jesus is Lord, not us. The Great Commission of Jesus tells us to "go" into the world under his authority and reign, not to grasp it for ourselves (vv. 19–20). And so we enter our neighborhoods as friends, just as God did in Christ, in humility, "emptying" ourselves of privileged status, becoming servants (Phil. 2:5–8). We enter the world to make space for God to work. Wherever we are, we submit to his rule. We sit, we pray, we listen, and then we ask questions. God is present in the world, working. He will be the one judging people. The minute the church seeks to grasp hold of God's power in Christ, his presence and power is no longer among us. God would not be God if he could be controlled by me or you. We must be totally dependent on him, listening and discerning his work in the world so that we, as his subjects, can participate with him in his mission in the world.[15]

Obviously I should not enable or support actions I know can harm my son. I may be able to discourage him from pursuing destructive behavior, but in the end, my teenager is starting to think for himself. I must honor that. That is love. And so in conversation, in relationship, my son will become more and more his own person, owning his thought, thinking through who he is, discovering all God has made him and called him to be. None of this can be done in the space of enemy making.

In the same way, every church in the world is to give witness to what God is doing in the world. Every chance we get as we are with people, we take time to be *with* people, alongside them, listening, observing, and, when appropriate, pointing to where God is at work in their lives. We may say, "I believe I see God at work in that. Do you see it too?" But we are not in charge. God will do the saving. We do not judge. We do not try to convince people of sin. God will convict people of their sin through the Spirit (John 16:8). God will do the judging. God's presence is enough. We leave room for God's wrath to be worked out (through the withdrawal of his presence),[16] but we never avenge. Vengeance is the Lord's (Rom. 12:19). In all these ways the church lives beyond enemies.

No Enemies?

But once again we come to this question: Can a church really be a witness to the gospel if it is making no enemies? How can a church speak truth on issues of injustice in its neighborhood without offending people?

The answer to these questions requires that we again distinguish between making enemies and revealing enemies. The very presence of Christ disrupts a social context and reveals enemies. Jesus acknowledged as much when he said, "I have not come to bring peace, but a sword" (Matt. 10:34). But the sword, we remember, is not a violent sword but the sword of his Word.[17] His very presence, accompanied by his persuasive Word, reveals enemies for the purpose of making space for the unwinding of antagonisms, for presence, healing, and restored relationship with God and one another.

So in the same chapter of Matthew, Jesus sends out his disciples into the towns and villages to "cure the sick, raise the dead, cleanse the lepers, cast out demons" (Matt. 10:8). He tells them to go, enter a home, and if welcomed, make space for his peace (v. 13). In other words, he is telling them to make space for his presence.

But he knows his presence will disrupt. The disciples represent Jesus, so their mere presence will make those comfortable with injustice uncomfortable. He warns the disciples of this (v. 14). In the midst of his presence, there will eventually be a clarifying moment when enemies are revealed. His disciples are not to try and control these circumstances. Just leave and move on. Shake the dust off your feet (v. 14). God will be the judge, not you (v. 15). We must go on humbly to the next place as sheep among wolves (v. 16). And we expect our very presence in Christ to disrupt the people in that place too.

And so as we enter the world, we can expect "all hell to break loose." Relationships will be disrupted (v. 22). We will be brought before the authorities (v. 18). Demons will protest. We must expect this. But this is not of our own doing. This antagonism was there before we arrived. The disruption is the first step toward unwinding it, and when disruption comes, we must stay in it, being present to what God is doing. We speak in the words of the Spirit, not our own prepared speeches (v. 20). We need to do nothing more than persevere (v. 22), be faithful.

Jesus's presence, therefore, does not make enemies; it reveals them. In his peaceful presence Jesus promises that "nothing is covered up that will not be uncovered, and nothing secret that will not become known" (v. 26). Antagonisms, chaos, hate, vitriol, and violence are all signs of *the enemy* at work. They are the source of his power. And yet Satan disguises it all in the name of piety and self-righteousness. But Satan is revealed in the unanxious presence of the living Lord. Satan's powers are disarmed. Though Jesus's presence is not violent, nonetheless in his presence the antagonisms are slowly disrupted, unwound, allowing us to turn, repent, find the love and forgiveness of Jesus, and enter the new world of the King. This is the way God works in what can only be described as the space beyond enemies. The question is, Can the church be this space in the world? Can we be the church that is beyond "us vs. them"?

One night, amid the flames and bullets, the violence and hate, the members of Koinonia Farm asked themselves, Is it time to leave? Clarence Jordan answered, "Shall we go off and leave them without hope? We have too many enemies to leave them."[18] Jordan was saying, ironically, the enemies of Christ have been revealed through our presence. Now that we know they are enemies, we cannot leave them. We must invite our enemies into reconciliation, forgiveness, restoration, and being loved. This is the way God shall heal the world. This is the space beyond us vs. them.

Moving beyond Enemies in Our Politics

Several years ago a widowed man named Alan came to me, as his pastor, and told me that a woman named Deirdre had reported him to the Department of Children and Family Services. Both were members of our church. Alan had been homeschooling his two children as a widower. Deirdre had wonderfully come to the aid of the family, helping Alan care for the children when he couldn't be home and teaching the children when he was too busy. One day Dierdre, a professional social worker, offered Alan an assessment of the children and told him that he was missing the mark and was doing an inadequate job of caring for the children's needs. John disagreed. He was offended and refused her advice. Deirdre decided on her own that the children were at risk, and as a professional, she reported Alan to the DCFS. A conflict broke out. Alan asked me as pastor to "get Deirdre in line." Deirdre told the pastors this was an emergency situation and she had no choice.

The three pastors of our church, myself included, all at different times, asked them to come together, to meet face-to-face and listen to one another and, in the spirit of Matthew 18:15–20, discern this disagreement. Each time they would say, more or less, "No thanks. I'm right; he/she is wrong. Please tell him/her what to do." Finally, after several weeks and multiple sincere invitations to both of them, they both agreed to meet. But as one of the pastors explained the process, that we would all submit our lives to Christ and to one another and listen for what God wanted to do, Deirdre got uneasy. She said, "Do you mean this meeting could result in me being wrong?" The pastor said "yes," and she said, "I'm out!"

What was apparent was that they were both entering into this space as a contest that could have only one clear winner. There was no sense of a space beyond enemies, where Jesus was present, and where we were discerning where God was taking us together in caring for our children.[19] Their egos were on the line. No matter what happened, one would come out a winner and one would come out a loser. And since their identities had become so wrapped up in the narrative of this argument, she as an expert social worker and he as a good father, neither could risk being wrong. This meeting would either affirm or not affirm who they were as persons. For them to learn from each other was impossible.

This had all the markings of the enemy-making machine. We have seen these things before, but we also know that, amid every conflict, Jesus invites us into another way. He instructs us at the outset of the conflict to go directly to the person and tell them how they have sinned against us (Matt. 18:15). Go meet face-to-face. Don't turn the other person into an object. Deal with the issue of grievance directly. Don't make it into a banner. Submit yourself and your identity to his lordship ("in my name" [v. 20]). See if you will be listened to. Do this as a community. Open space (vv. 16–17). Discern this together. And when you come to an agreement, it is not as if somebody wins and somebody loses. His very presence has entered this place (v. 20). Indeed, the very rule and reign of the King has been invoked. "Whatever you bind on earth will be bound in heaven, and whatever you loose on earth will be loosed in heaven" (v. 18).[20] This is truly a place beyond enemies. This is the politics of Jesus. It is beyond me vs. you, beyond the church of us vs. them. Yet Alan and Deirdre said no. They couldn't see that this disagreement was about so much more than who was right or wrong in their particular spat.

Leading churches into this new politics of the kingdom will therefore take leaders who can describe what God is doing in the space beyond enemies. We must lead people in conflict into his presence. We must proclaim his lordship in and over every conflict. It will take persistent, patient, and noncoercive leadership. I believe God wanted to use the conflict between Alan and Deirdre to teach our church about caring for our children and caring for the widower, how to look at and see our children, how to care for the children in our neighborhoods, even in our state and country. They could have been used to begin a revolution of his kingdom, but Alan and Deirdre were not able to see this vision of church.

Apart from practicing this form of local kingdom politics, the church cannot engage the institutions and systems that govern our lives. Until a church itself can become the space beyond enemies, it cannot be the space beyond enemies in the world. It's merely another instance of the church of us vs. them. Just as Alan and Deirdre got caught up in the enemy-making machine, so also a church can get caught up in taking sides in local city-hall disputes or national elective politics. In so doing, it misses the opportunities to discern where God is taking each local church in relation to the issues of injustice actually occurring in our neighborhoods.

Jesus's disciples did not come from any one political party. Among the disciples were publicans (who sided with Rome), zealots (who wanted a violent takedown of Rome), and even Essenes (ascetics who wanted to withdraw from Rome). Following Jesus shook to the core all of their political loyalties. Jesus instead called them to a way of life, the new politic of the kingdom: his reign, a politic that was beyond anything they could imagine in human terms. This takes us beyond the church of us vs. them. This is the way beyond enemies.

Fullness

Most people know the difference between a full stomach and an empty one. Some of us also know the difference between eating healthy food and eating junk food. The first, devoid of added sugar, often energizes you in a way that goes on and on through the rest of the day. After you've eaten healthy food, you're full in a good way. The second gives you an immediate high but then leaves you drained. After you've eaten junk food, you might feel full, but that feeling is illusory. When you've eaten well and your body feels energetic, you can give yourself to tasks in a seemingly endless flow. Your energy is boundless. If you've eaten junk, you might soon end up with a sugar low, and that's when things can get really ugly. Grouchiness sets in as you defend yourself from anyone who may be challenging you or needing something from you. Depleted of energy, you're just looking to find some real food fast (but not fast food!) so you can survive. This is why I try to eat healthy whenever I can.

A church can be full, living in and through the abundance of God's presence in Jesus Christ. Or it can be empty, living on bursts of highs and lows of its own energy and achievement yet finding itself exhausted. A church can live in submission to God's unique presence in Jesus, giving and receiving his great gifts. Out of this presence, the church can overflow with his love into the world, able to attend to his presence in the world and thereby giving, serving, and participating in God's mission. Or a church can live on its own energy. Often it must turn inward in order to try to conserve its energy. It starts to see other churches' goals as in competition with its own. Such a church often finds itself talking about the enemies it faces in its culture, even in other churches. It actually draws energy by organizing against an enemy! But this energy, like a bad sugar high, soon depletes and leaves the church needing another enemy to keep it going. The first church describes what a "politic of fullness" looks like. The second church is what I call an "empty politic," empty at the core, with only the enemy-making machine to keep it going.[21]

In Ephesians 1, Paul describes the church with the word "fullness." He describes how God has made Jesus "head over all things for the church, which is his body, the *fullness* of him" (vv. 22–23). New Testament scholar Markus Barth says this word "fullness," *pleroma* in the Greek, describes how "God fills his house on earth with his presence, so that his 'fullness' resides at the chosen place and manifests itself with power."[22] It is an allusion to the shekinah glory of God's presence in the Holy of Holies in the temple of Israel.[23] And yet God's presence is not confined to the location of the church, for the apostle immediately follows "the fullness of him" with "who fills all in all" (v. 23). And so the difference between God's presence in the church and God's presence in the world is one of intensity. God is present everywhere, throughout the whole world. But his presence is intense, becoming manifest, made visible, in the church.

A. W. Tozer describes this same dynamic when he says God's *omnipresence* is over the whole world but his *manifest presence* is seen in the lives of Christians.[24] Going beyond Tozer's focus on individual Christians, the apostle Paul's point in Ephesians is that God manifests his presence through Christ in a people, the local church. Though he is omnipresent over the whole world, his presence becomes visibly manifest wherever Christians gather as Christ's local body.

And so we gather in his presence around the communion table. We give thanks, we open our lives to him, we hear his Word

preached, and we are full. We gather around tables in neighborhoods to tend to his presence. There too, we know his forgiveness
anew, his reconciliation, his strength and enabling, his healing,
his renewal of all things, and we can see this visibly in a people
dwelling in his presence. We submit to his presence in the various
gifts. In so doing we grow into his fullness (Eph. 4:13). We live out
of this abundance. No longer a space of chaos (v. 14), we grow
into his full body (v. 16). We become his fullness.

This is so different from the space of enemy making we have
become accustomed to. This is the way of abundance, and its overflow leads us into the world to discern his presence there. This is
what it means to live the politic of fullness in Jesus Christ.

A New Way of Doing Church

This way of seeing church changes how we do church. As in Acts
2:46–47, the church gathers in God's presence (1) in the close circle
of his fullness ("the temple"), but it also gathers regularly (2) in
the neighborhood through the sharing of food and fellowship ("at
home" or "from house to house") and (3) in the spaces among the
hurting and lost ("having the goodwill of *all* the people"). This
way of doing church requires that people cultivate a way of life
that tends to his presence in all three places of everyday life. Such
a church will de-emphasize programs and spend time creating
spaces of his presence among people in the world. We will see the
Sunday gathering as a place of his intense presence that enables
us to discern his presence in the other circles of our lives. We will
inhabit the various places of our lives to discern and witness to his
presence. We will inhabit homeless shelters, gymnasiums, schools,
community centers, village committee meetings, community po-
licing groups, bars, restaurants, places of work, hospitals, prisons,
commuter trains, and grocery-store coffee shops as places where
God is already present, although in some cases not yet recognized.
We will make space for his presence to become manifest!

We will move from churches as efficient and effective organizations to churches as patient places that cultivate the kingdom.
We will move from centrally organized senior leadership being
responsible for the entirety of church operations to a polycentric
leadership that unleashes leaders and the gifts of the Holy Spirit
into every nook and cranny of the places where we live. Such
leaders will see every conflict as the place from which the Spirit
will move. In these and many other ways, seeing church differently
changes how we do church.[25]

As We Go into the World

Compare a typical political rally in the United States to a local
church gathering around the Lord's table on any given Sunday
morning. In today's political rally, it is common to hear candidates
make speeches that work the crowd into a frenzy. A candidate
says very little about the goals, vision, or actual policy proposals
he or she stands for. The rally instead often turns into an overt
attack on the candidate's opponent through the use of deroga-
tory speech and catchphrases that stir up the crowd, and often in
a way that objectifies the opponent as disgusting or evil. Chants
like "Lock her up!" and "Racist!" are painfully common at today's
political rallies. Certainly this is not true of all candidates, but
the prevalence of this kind of political rally in the last few years
in the United States is undeniable.

Switch gears now to the local church gathering around the
Lord's table on Sunday morning. The presiding minister steps into
the midst of the gathering. We share the peace of Christ. As we
gather in his presence, there can be no antagonisms here because
his presence unwinds antagonisms. We therefore must come to
this table "discerning" our relationships both to Jesus as Lord
and with each other. Is there any enmity between us? Make sure
to reconcile before coming to the table.[26] The presiding leader
starts with a prayer of thanksgiving (often called the Eucharistic

prayer). We give thanks to God for all he has done, from creation to the sending of his Son. This "giving thanks" opens our arms to receive from God. It is such a different posture than looking to defend ourselves over against someone else. The pastor prays a prayer of *epiclesis*: "Lord, make your presence real to us."[27] The body of Christ is broken, his blood poured out, and the forgiveness of sin, together with the reconciliation, healing, and renewal of all things, flows forth in this new relationship with God through Jesus Christ. What is referred to as "the gifts of God for the people of God" is an abundance that comes from who God is.

The political rally, in contrast, depends on the making of an enemy to stir the crowd. The ones who gather gain their identity by being against something. If you took away that enemy, the crowd would fritter away because there would be nothing left for them to gather around. Their life would be empty at the core. This politic shapes us as an angry, coercive, and defensive people.

The church, however, comes together around the presence of the living God. This presence comes as an overflowing gift through the incarnate Christ becoming present by the Spirit among this people. This presence offers forgiveness, reconciliation, healing, and renewal by the Spirit. It transforms relationships in a face-to-face encounter. The reality of his fullness is present wherever we gather because he comes in flesh and blood, the body and blood, broken and raised for all. Its resources are infinite because God is infinite. Its core is full and unending. This politic shapes us as a peaceful people, a people of invitation and generosity to the world, a people beyond enemies, a church beyond us vs. them.

The question for Christians everywhere, as we gather in church services amid the tumult of our times, is this: Is my church more like a political rally or the table of the Lord? Is our life together "empty" at the core or do we gather in his fullness? Do we gather as a church of us vs. them or as one body in Christ? Can we, by the power and presence of the living Christ, be that space in the world that is beyond enemies?

9

beyond the church of us vs. them

The Robbers Cave experiment of 1954 is an allegory for what we're facing as Christians in North America. Muzafer Sherif, a social psychologist, organized a camp for twenty-two boys at Robbers Cave State Park in Oklahoma. He laid out the campground so that there would be two cabins, each sleeping eleven campers plus a counselor. The cabins were far enough apart that each side could not see or hear the other. Each had its own swimming, boating, and recreational areas. The campers were all the same age (eleven years old), came from similar socioeconomic and church backgrounds, and had similar grades in school. When they arrived at the campground, they were immediately separated into two groups that occupied the two different cabins. Each group participated in its own activities collectively.

By the end of the first week, the campers had become two very distinct groups with their own leaders, rules for behavior, and names (the Rattlers and the Eagles). Beginning in the second week, the campers were allowed to run into each other around the campground. At one point, both of the groups wanted to play baseball at the one baseball diamond in the campground, and an argument broke out. This began a pattern. They challenged one another regularly in sports and other competitions.

According to Sherif, an us vs. them mentality took over the two groups of eleven-year-olds. Name-calling ensued. One side burned the flag of the other side, and the act was reciprocated by the other side. They raided each other's cabins at night, turning over beds and ripping mosquito netting. One night, the Rattlers and the Eagles met for an all-out fistfight, complete with sticks, bats, and socks filled with stones. Had it not been for the counselors stepping in, surely there would have been injuries.

In the last stage of the experiment, the experimenters tried to bring the two sides together. They planned casual get-togethers like watching movies and eating meals together. Group members continued to call each other names, throw food at each other, and refuse to associate with those on the other side. Nothing changed until a series of crises, produced by the experimenters, forced the Rattlers and the Eagles to work together. When their drinking water was blocked, for instance, the two groups had to work together to unblock the water at its source and release its flow back into the pipes. When they ran low on supplies and it was about to rain, the two sides had to quickly pool their resources to eat an adequate meal and get through the night. Each time they joined together for a common goal, they would grow closer. It is not incidental, I suggest, that they came together over food. By joining together over the making of a meal (among other things), the hostility was eventually overcome and they became friends.

In the years since the study, many have wondered what to think of the controversial experiment and where its findings point us.[1] Some say it just proves that tribalism is an inescapable fact of human life: deal with it. Others suggest it proves groups can only overcome tribalism when a crisis happens: never waste a good crisis; use it to bring people together. Some just admit that groups only come together around a common enemy: there's nothing that can change that. Looking at the current state of our churches, one wonders whether we've entered our own version of the Robbers Cave experiment.

Whatever the issues—whether related to race, sexuality, religious pluralism, abortion, immigration, or any of a host of other political agenda items at local, state, and federal levels— our churches seem condemned to the bad habits of enemy making and group-identity formation around antagonisms. And the kinds of people we've become, prone to be arrogant, judgmental, duplicitous, angry, and vindictive, has sapped our witness of its power. Fewer and fewer people want to know us, and even fewer want to be us. Our way of life has become unattractive to the average North American.

And so we ask, like many did after Robbers Cave, Is there a way beyond the church of us vs. them? Can we move beyond the enemy-making machines of Christendom, the tribalisms of our history, to become a people of God for his mission? Can we become the reconciling presence of Jesus in the world? Can we become the space beyond enemies?

A New Practice of Church

Like gathering together to eat a meal at Robbers Cave, a new practice of church that gathers us together as a people beyond enemies lies within this book. Seamlessly tied to a deeper understanding of our core beliefs, this new practice is a way of being a people that moves from enemy making to making space for the presence of Christ to be manifest among us in the world. Like eating a meal at his table, this new practice gathers us into his fullness, not the emptiness of being defined by what we are against. It is the space beyond enemies, beyond the church of us vs. them.

In this space, the Bible is God's Grand Drama, conversion is the entry into his lordship and all he is doing to draw the world to himself, and church is the local politic of his fullness, that which makes visible his kingdom, his manifest presence, into which the world can be challenged and even invited. This space forces us to relearn how we read the Bible together, how we preach the Bible, how we evangelize, how we disciple, and how we think about, lead, and do church. The Bible, conversion, and church-culture politics no longer divide us. Instead, as our practices surrounding all three change in this way, space is opened up in which we submit to one another in the fullness of Christ, and his kingdom breaks out. The Bible, conversion, and the church itself draw us deeper into his fullness, a space beyond enemies.

But perhaps most poignantly, in the post–Willow Creek era of church, these ways of believing reshape the way we lead church.[2] For as we lead into seeing the Bible differently, broadening and deepening the salvation we are inviting the world into, and challenging today's divisive politics with a living alternative politic of the local church, we will surely arouse the antagonisms that drive so much of the church and the world today. It will be so easy to get caught up into these antagonisms. How will we lead into this space beyond enemies so that we ourselves are not caught up into the enemy-making machine?

Neither Do I Condemn Thee

Jesus provides us a model for this kind of leadership in John 8:2–11.[3] A woman caught in adultery is placed before the mob ("making her stand before all of them" [v. 3]). She has been made into an object, "the enemy," for the enemy-making machine, and the crowd are now directing their collective wrath toward her. There is no relational space between the people of the mob and the woman toward whom they are aiming their fury. And so, although she stands before them, they ask Jesus a question about her as if she is not even present and does not count as a human being. They have made her into a depersonalized object and have distanced themselves from her so that they can aim their perverse anger at her.

In the midst of the spectacle, they ask Jesus whether this woman should be stoned as "in the law Moses commanded" (v. 5). A belief system, "the law" as given by God to be concretely lived out in the covenantal life of Israel's community, has become a banner to get behind. Instead of a sign of new life for the world, it is now used to pit one group of people against another, to define who is in and who is out. It has become an ideology of self-righteousness in which the Pharisees find their identity and feel good about themselves. There's some perverse self-congratulatory enjoyment at work here as they are able to say that she failed while they themselves are holy and keep the law. These are all signs of the enemy-making machine at work. Jesus is asked to enter smack-dab into the middle of the enemy-making machine and take a side.

Strikingly, Jesus is silent. He stoops down to write on the ground. This kind of tactic, using silence and distraction, is one that Jesus uses repeatedly throughout the Gospels when he is presented with similar circumstances. It is stunning how often he refuses to enter into the violence of his culture on the terms offered to him by the ideology. And so we too must become present to the conflicts of our churches (and the world) while quietly refusing to enter on the terms given by the enemy-making machines of the world. We come unanxiously, willing to take on the insults ourselves. We might use a tactic to distract as Jesus did to resist the antagonism. As Jesus did, we too can engage in the tactics of the weak, as a people not in power on the world's terms but humbly witnessing to another power: the presence of the living Lord.[4]

Jesus then suggests, "Let anyone among you who is without sin be the first to throw a stone at her" (v. 7). He is saying provocatively, "OK, obviously you are righteous and perfect enough to stand in judgment against her—which is contradictory itself. So by all means, go ahead and stone her!" It again is a tactic, the tactic of seeking agreement first in a manner that brings to the surface the underlying contradictions at work. Banners, in the enemy-making machine, often cover over the contradictions at work in the conflict. By agreeing, and then taking the underlying assumptions to their extreme, this duplicity can be revealed. Often, such a tactic exposes the perverse enjoyment going on as well. Here the perverse enjoyment at work in the Pharisees who want to stone the woman is exposed. The ones ready to stone the woman suddenly see themselves in the absurdity of the moment. The antagonism is broken and the violence flitters away as one by one the accusers disperse. The woman is left in the presence of Jesus, cleared of all the strife and violence and anger.

Jesus often asks questions as a tactic to reveal the contradictions at work in the people's assumptions. We remember how he was being questioned once about paying taxes by the religious authorities trying to trap him (Luke 20:22). He again answered with a question. The NIV translation of Luke 20:23–24 says that "he saw through their duplicity" and then asked, "Show me a denarius. Whose image and inscription are on it?" His questions were meant to draw out the assumptions, expose the perverse enjoyments so people could see themselves, and then open space for real people-to-people encounters for the kingdom.

In the same way as Jesus, we too must refuse to enter the violence of the world's antagonisms on the terms offered by the antagonism. We must be present, unanxious, taking in the insults, asking good questions, allowing the contradictions and perverse glee to be exposed. Only after all this has dissipated, and Jesus can ask "Woman, where are your accusers?" (my paraphrase of v. 10), is space cleared for Jesus to work. Simply by doing this, we peacefully disrupt the enemy-making machine and make space for the presence of Christ to become real so true healing and reconciliation can begin.

And so, after the woman is released from the violence of hate and antagonism, Jesus does say, "You are forgiven. You are free. Now go in the way of righteousness, and choose sin no more.

Work out in community what it means to become whole in the power of the Spirit" (my paraphrase of the dynamics of John 8:11). Indeed, this is only possible for the woman after she has been freed from the ideological enemy-making machine. Because there can be no healing in the enemy-making machine. It must be unwound. But once the scribes and Pharisees have left, Jesus can reassert the true sense of the law. He does not throw away orthodoxy; he extends its true intent into the life of this woman.

This episode is a picture of the church that has been moved beyond the enemy-making machine of "us vs. them." This church is the presence of Christ in the world of antagonisms we are living in. This presence of Jesus unwinds the vitriol, anger, and violence of the enemy-making machine. His presence makes space for the dismantling of the world of the enemy. In him the church is released from the enemy-making machine's grasp and true healing comes. In Jesus, space is opened for the healing of the world.

This is the challenge of this book: Can my church be this Jesus in my neighborhood? Gifted with a new practice of reading and preaching the Scripture together, a broader and deeper practice of conversion and mission, a thicker and fuller way of being his church in the world, can we become his reconciling presence in the world full of strife all around us where we live? Can we make space for his presence in our own lives and in the lives of those around us? Can we be used by God to bring his healing, transforming power into the world? "For he himself is our peace" (Eph. 2:14 NIV).

Appendix 1

the fullness of him
who fills all in all

Rudiments of a Political Theology of Presence

I n the book of Ephesians, the apostle describes the church (Christ's "body") as "the fullness of him who fills all in all" (Eph. 1:23). This text, in one sentence, summarizes a profound theology of the church's presence in the world. It places the church, as Christ's presence ("the fullness of him"), in the very center of Christ's presence ("who fills all in all") over the whole world. This in turn implies a dynamic relationship between the church and the world. The text further entails a certain view of the way God uses the church as an instrument of his mission in the world. And finally, I would argue, the text assumes a certain understanding of power and the way God works in the world. In short, although it is always dangerous to place too much weight on a single text, this text provides a stunning summary of how the church gathers as his presence in the world that is already filled by his presence. It is a political theology of presence. Let's examine it one piece at a time.

The Politic of His Fullness versus an Empty Politic

First, notice how Ephesians 1:23 declares the church to be his "fullness" in the midst of the whole world (perhaps even the entire cosmos), which he also "fills all in all." The church and the world are both places filled by his presence. As we learned in chapter 8, "fullness," in this text, is an allusion to the shekinah glory of God's presence in the Holy of Holies in the temple of Israel.[1] Implied here is that God is viscerally present in the gathering of God's people in Christ, just as he was present in the temple. And yet God's presence is not confined to the location of the church, for his presence "fills all in all." So the difference between Christ's presence in the church and his presence in the rest of the world is a matter of intensity. He is present over (and in) the whole world, yet Christ manifests his presence in "fullness" among his church, wherever Christians gather in submission to his rule.

As I have written elsewhere, "fullness" makes for a politic that is radically different from the politic that exists in the world in autonomy from God.[2] As opposed to a group gathered around and assenting to an idea (or belief), so that it in essence becomes a "cause," this group gathers in his fullness and submits to him and his presence together. A mutuality among a people results that is at the core of this politic in his fullness. His presence gathers people to live what we believe out of relationship. There is still common belief among these people, but it is belief practiced out of relationship. This is so different from when we gather as individuals and assent to a belief in an autonomous act that is prone to antagonism.

There is an abundance, a plenty, an overflow from God in this space of fullness. In the space of autonomy (from God), however, with no source of ultimate provision, living in a world of scarcity, we are bent toward organizing ourselves to defend and maintain our lives over against others. We in essence organize around an antagonism. It is empty at the core around which we gather, because what drives us is what we are against, not the fullness of his presence out of which we live our lives. This "empty politic" is built on finding our identity against the other, fighting to defend what we have materially. Whereas the fullness of God overflows with generosity into the world, the empty politic distances those of us who gather in it from those we are organized against.

Both the empty politic and the politic of fullness require subjects if there is to truly be a social group. In the politic of fullness, we become subjects by submitting mutually to one another in his presence. We gather in his name (Matt. 18:15–20). Jesus is Lord here. There is no usurping one over another in this politic (Luke 22:25–27). God's presence is noncoercive, so we must open space for his rule. We must submit to him together in order for his presence to be made known among us. We do this via historic practices given to us by Christ, such as the historic sacramental practices of the church.[3] In so doing, we are grafted into his people and find our location in his mission for the world, for his presence here among us enables us to discern him in the world.

The empty politic, on the other hand, creates its subjects through the stirring of anger and antagonism. The individual is subjectivized by finding his or her identity in the cause. This cause, however, is not grounded in the incarnation of God in the fullness of the Son. This cause is extracted out of the world (ex-carnation) and creates or identifies an enemy. The individual recognizes himself or herself in the cause and joins in against the enemy.

As a result, striving is increased via the empty politic. It characterizes the empty politic. People caught up in its swirl take swipes at other people, compare what they have to what others have, always see their circumstances in terms of lack rather than abundance. These people live in a state of perpetual discontent. In contrast, in the politic of fullness, God asks us to cease our striving, to "be still" and know his presence as real (Ps. 46:10). It is in this space, the space beyond enemies, where he can come to be present and work for forgiveness, reconciliation, healing, perseverance and abundance in sufferings, and the renewal of all things.

In 1 Corinthians 3, the apostle Paul points to the church's quarrels as a signal that the church is not yet living into the space of God's presence. He says that taking sides by saying "I belong to Apollos" or "I belong to Paul" is a sign of living in "the flesh, and behaving according to human inclinations," apart from God (1 Cor. 3:3–4). The church at Corinth has lapsed into the empty politic. A few verses later, Paul asks them, "Do you not know that you are God's temple and that God's Spirit dwells in you [plural]?" (v. 16). The antagonism and striving are signs that the church of Corinth has abandoned living into the fullness of his presence for the empty politic of antagonism.

This does not mean there will never be conflict in the church of his fullness—quite the contrary, in fact.[4] But conflict, in the politic of fullness, will be the means by which the church comes together in his presence rather than the means for it to be torn apart into sides. Here, we will not make enemies of others. We will not derive our identity from taking sides. We will not abstract conflicts and make banners of them to make war against each other. We will not take pleasure in anyone's demise. Instead, in every conflict, we ask, What is God doing here? What is he teaching me about myself? Where is he taking us? Every conflict then becomes an opportunity for mutual submission to his presence together in a practice of reconciliation and discernment. Every conflict is a turning point for a decision: Will we gather in his fullness, or will we devolve into the quarreling that is so typical of the life together devoid of his presence (the empty politic)?

It could not be any clearer then: the church's presence in the world is defined by its gathering into Christ's fullness. It alone is capable of a politic of fullness among the world because it alone is his body, the space of his presence made manifest among a people.

From the church, life overflows into the world of God's mission to restore the whole world to his presence. To gather in his fullness places us in the midst of the world, making space for his presence to become visible for the world to see. To live the empty politic puts the church into an antagonistic relation with the world. It separates the church from the world and from his mission by setting us up within the life of antagonism. In the current climate of North American culture, we can imagine just how powerful a witness to the world it would be for the church to live into the politic of Christ's fullness.

The Temple as Metaphor for the Church as His Fullness

As we have already seen, the apostle Paul declares that the church is God's temple and that God's Spirit dwells uniquely in it (1 Cor. 3:16; 2 Cor. 6:16). The temple of Israel is a metaphor for the way God's presence is central to who the church is and the way it must inhabit the world in God's mission. And yet the worry is that to see the church as the locus of God's presence in this way is to somehow make God's presence exclusive to the church.[5] This would in turn set the church apart from the world and God in mission. A closer look, however, helps us see that any time where Israel in its history claims the temple for its own possession is a denial of its calling and a lapse into the empty politic, setting it against the nations. Instead, the temple is the basis for Israel pushing into the world for God's mission.

This is substantiated by Hebrew scholar Jon Levenson. The temple in the Old Testament, according to Levenson, is built to be a microcosm of the entire universe. The temple is not a place that houses God's presence to the exclusion of the world. On the contrary, according to Levenson, from this temple, God "is manifesting his presence throughout the world."[6] In Isaiah 6, for example, the smoke of his presence filled the temple (v. 4); nonetheless, "the whole earth is full of his glory" (v. 3). God's fullness in the temple does not negate his presence over the whole world. It is the place from which he makes his presence known (as it exists in the whole world) to the rest of the world. Levenson describes the Jewish perception of the temple as the "navel of God's creation" from which he is re-creating the world. The temple, then, was never meant to be a place to confine the presence of God to Jerusalem. For what building can contain the presence of the living God (1 Kings 8:27)? Rather, the temple was the place from which God would make known his presence in and over the whole world.

In similar fashion, New Testament scholar G. K. Beale shows that God's intention, from the beginning of the Bible to the end, was to extend his presence over the whole earth. The temple is foundational to this mission of God over all the earth. According to Beale (and others), the Garden of Eden was created and described (dimensionally) in Genesis as a temple for God's presence. The fall happened. Sin entered the world. But God continued his mission to extend his presence over the whole earth. The calling of his people Israel and the building of the ark of the covenant, the tabernacle, and then the temple were all part of God's restoring his presence to humanity. When the failures of Israel and the destruction of the temple happened, again, God nonetheless persisted in this same mission. So he sent the Son, "Emmanuel, God with us," to be present and restore humanity to God's presence. Revelation 21 is a picture of the culmination of this mission. Here the writer describes the new heavens and the new earth, where there shall be no more temple (v. 22). Indeed, the new Jerusalem is itself the completion of the temple as the place where God fully dwells with humanity (v. 3).[7]

In light of this, it is no surprise that the apostle Paul calls the church "God's temple" (1 Cor. 3:16) and uses the word "fullness" (*pleroma*) to describe the church, alluding to the shekinah glory of God's presence in the temple of the Old Testament (Eph. 1:23).[8] For Paul, every church, like Israel's temple, gathers in God's manifest presence wherever they meet. From this place, his fullness extends into the world as the church makes space for God's presence to become visible. Through his people, God's presence becomes known over the whole world. It is a politic of fullness.

Centripetal or Centrifugal?

This kind of politic of fullness, viewed via the metaphor of the temple, changes the way we understand the relation between the church and the world in mission. Some might infer that the temple metaphor suggests the church/world dynamic is centripetal, with the world moving toward the church, just as the nations are sometimes pictured as streaming to Zion (Isa. 2:2; Mic. 4:2). The Word goes out and calls the world to come to the church.

This dynamic of the world moving toward the church as center is certainly part of the way the church works in the world. One of the more positive ways to view this centripetal dynamic is through missiologist Paul Hiebert's concept of "bounded set" and "centered set." Understanding the church/world distinction through a bounded-set lens sees the church as only those who have crossed God's boundary to be his forgiven people. The world are those who have not yet crossed the boundary into being God's people. The key question for this view is, Are you inside or outside of the boundary? In contrast, understanding the church/world distinction via the centered-set concept sees all people as either moving toward the center, Jesus Christ, or moving away from him. The key question for this view is, What direction are you heading and how can I guide, help, and support you toward knowing the God of our Lord Jesus Christ more fully?[9] The centered-set view, as distinct from the bounded-set view, helps explain the centripetal movement of the world toward the temple and how that works in mission.

Levenson and Beale, however, via their analysis of temple, add a second dimension to this church/world dynamic in mission. For both Levenson and Beale, the temple was not merely a gateway from the world to God but was indeed the gateway from God into the world. Never was it assumed that God was only present in the temple or that God was not present in the world. Rather, the temple was the means by which God would extend his manifest visible presence over the whole world. God's purpose was to make the whole earth his temple, his dwelling place with all of humanity (Rev. 21).

What this means, then, is that there is both a centripetal and a centrifugal movement between the church and the world. Indeed, we are not only concerned with the direction of people's lives toward the center, and a deeper, more intense knowing of the presence of the living Christ in a social space. We are equally concerned with the move outward by Christians into the world, discerning his presence at work in the world and making space for him to become visible in the lives and circumstances of those living outside the knowledge of his lordship. The politic of fullness thus sees the movement of the church in the world as dialogical, both centripetal and centrifugal.

The church moves into the world while at the same time the world moves toward the church. God is present over the whole earth, and the church must go there to make space in the world for God's presence to be made known. And yet the Grand Drama of God drawing the whole world into his presence draws people to him and his fullness via the church, which is on this mission. A centrifugal move outward from the church makes way for a new centripetal draw into God's Story and mission. In this way the church is "the fullness of him who fills all in all" (Eph. 1:23).

Presence versus Antagonism

Lastly, when we see the church's location in the world via his fullness, this shapes the very posture and mode of engagement of the church in the world. Presence, by its very nature, is non-violent. There is no striving in the presence of God. There can be no antagonism. Rather, as we enter the world, our one task is to go, be with, and make space in the world for his presence to be recognized. When two or three gather and submit to his name in trust and faith, a space is opened where God's power and presence can be manifest. As we sit with those who do not yet recognize God, or have even rejected him, God works through disruption to become present when his people are there to give witness. In this presence is a unique kind of power. This power is not coercive; it does not usurp. Rather, through the Spirit, we discern, his gifts are set loose, and God works through his presence in and among us to reshape the world.[10]

It is into this politic of fullness that the church is called. It is the space beyond enemies. It can never be the church of us vs. them. It is this majestic politic lived in his fullness that is the instrument of the Triune God's work in the world.

To God be all the glory.

Appendix 2

tactics for engagement

Opening Space among the Antagonisms

1. **Tell a story about a real person. Then ask, How do we discern this issue?** Don't let things stay in the conceptual realm. Don't join in when the other is being demonized into an object of scorn. *"If any of you has a sheep and it falls into a pit on the Sabbath . . ."* *(Matt. 12:11)*.

2. **Make observations and ask questions that reveal the contradictions at work.** Don't make enemies (Matt. 12:25). Don't demonize the other. Open space. *"Whose image and inscription are on [this coin]?"* *(Luke 20:24)*.

3. **Do not humiliate or defeat the other person.** Reject winning as the goal. Seek friendship. *"If a brother or sister sins against you, go directly to him or her. If he or she listens, you have gained a friend"* *(Matt. 18:15; my translation)*.

4. **Start with agreement. Move from what we have in common to exposing the antagonism at work.** Sometimes by agreeing in excess we can see the absurdity. *"["Yes."] Let*

any one of you who is without sin be the first to throw a stone at her" (John 8:7).

5. **Make all proposals in the spirit of mutual submission.** Out of the recognition that Jesus is Lord and at work in this space, end each proposal with the words "I submit to you." Open space for the kingdom and for his Spirit to work. *"Submit to one another out of reverence for Christ" (Eph. 5:21).*

notes

Preface

1. David E. Fitch, *The End of Evangelicalism? Discerning a New Faithfulness for Mission* (Eugene, OR: Cascade Books, 2011).

Introduction Beyond Enemies?

1. Julia Ward Howe, "The Battle Hymn of the Republic," in *The Celebration Hymnal: Songs and Hymns for Worship* (n.p.: Word Music / Integrity Music, 1997), no. 804.

2. Peter Leithart, for one, gives an admirable positive assessment of denominationalism in North American Christianity in *The End of Protestantism* (Grand Rapids: Brazos, 2016), chap. 5.

3. In the vernacular of today's New Testament theologies, I'm saying that this space beyond enemies is both "apocalyptic" and "salvation-historical," both a radical break with what has gone on before (and therefore unexpected) and continuous with previous history (and therefore God's fulfillment of what he was working for in history all along). For a review and treatment of this issue in New Testament scholarship, see James H. Charlesworth, "Paul, the Jewish Apocalypses, and Apocalyptic Eschatology," in *Paul the Jew*, ed. Gabriele Boccaccini and Carlos Segovia (Minneapolis: Fortress, 2016), 83–106.

4. I have laid out this thesis extensively in my book *Faithful Presence: Seven Disciplines That Shape the Church for Mission* (Downers Grove, IL: IVP Books, 2016).

Chapter 2 The Enemy-Making Machine

1. Michael Emerson and Christian Smith observe this phenomenon as part of being in a pluralist society. They say, "Social groups construct and maintain collective identities by forming symbolic boundaries. . . . Groups must symbolize and

utilize symbolic boundaries to both create and give substance to shared values and identities. An in group always has at least one outgroup by which it creates identity." *Divided by Faith* (Oxford: Oxford University Press, 2001), 142–43. Much has been written in the past ten years in the field of sociology and political science about identity and groups. For a recent take, see Lilliana Mason, *Uncivil Agreement: How Politics Became Our Identity* (Chicago: University of Chicago Press, 2018).

2. I use the word "ideology" within the academic tradition of critical theory. From Marx to Lukács to Adorno to Althusser, the "critique of ideology" seeks to expose how groupthink works to keep some (the bourgeois) in power while others (the proletariat) serve those in power, thinking it was their own idea. From the study of ideology we learn how groups work, how they make enemies, and how they keep systems going. My own views on ideology and culture have been greatly influenced by the culture theorist/philosopher Slavoj Žižek. I have an extensive treatment of my appropriation of ideological theory in *The End of Evangelicalism? Discerning a New Faithfulness for Mission* (Eugene, OR: Cascade Books, 2011), chap. 2.

3. A fuller account of what I mean by "make space for Christ's manifest presence" can be found in my book *Faithful Presence: Seven Disciplines That Shape the Church for Mission* (Downers Grove, IL: IVP Books, 2016).

4. For those interested in an introduction to the current state of the critique of ideology within culture theory, I recommend Žižek's introduction to *Mapping Ideology*, ed. Slavoj Žižek (London: Verso Books, 1994), 1–34. See also Jan Rehman, *Theories of Ideology* (Chicago: Haymarket Books, 2014); Terry Eagleton, *Ideology: An Introduction* (London: Verso Books, 2007).

5. The notion of a "signifier" or "master signifier" or "empty signifier" draws from an extensive literature within post-structuralist political theory. I am drawing on political theorists Ernesto Laclau and Slavoj Žižek. See, for example, Ernesto Laclau, *Emancipation(s)* (London: Verso Books, 1996), chap. 3; Slavoj Žižek, *The Fragile Absolute: Or, Why Is the Christian Legacy Worth Fighting For?* (London: Verso Books, 2000), 114–15; Žižek, *The Indivisible Remainder: On Schelling and Related Matters* (London: Verso Books, 1996), 142.

6. Premillenial churches have tended to emphasize that the gospel must be preached "to all the nations . . . and then the end will come" (Matt. 24:14 NRSV). This has led to a world missions focus on taking the gospel to places ("nations") beyond the immediate contexts where the church already presumably is.

7. The way I describe the formation of the "enemy" is influenced by Žižek's description of the *objet petit a* via the work of social psychoanalyst Jacques Lacan. *Objet petit a* refers to the "small other," that piece of ourselves (called the "remainder") that keeps us from being complete. It is that lack in our "selves." This object keeps us striving for what completes us, but in fact we can never attain it, for if we did, we would have nothing to organize our selfhood around (or we'd have to invent something new). The example of "the Jew" in Nazi ideology is an example used again and again in this regard in Žižek's writing. See, for instance, Slavoj Žižek, *The Sublime Object of Ideology* (London: Verso Books, 1989), 124–25; *Fragile Absolute*, 48–50.

8. Žižek, in his political theory, labels this *jouissance*. A French word that is translated "perverse enjoyment," *jouissance* refers to excessive irrational enjoyments (often sexual in nature). Žižek uses it to describe the kind of enjoyment displaced toward an object that plays off resentment. This kind of enjoyment locks the subject into the grasp of the governing ideology. For one of Žižek's most concise treatments of this concept, see *Tarrying with the Negative: Kant, Hegel, and the Critique of Ideology* (Durham, NC: Duke University Press, 1993), 201–5.

9. The idea of one's identity/subjectivity as being located/founded within an ideology/discourse from whence one's feelings and desires get shaped blindly within the hold of that ideology/discourse was central to the work of French Marxist Louis Althusser and French post-structuralist Michel Foucault. Althusser's notion of "interpellation"—whereby a subject comes into being by being hailed within a power structure and/or an ideology—was groundbreaking in (and disruptive to) the post–World War II study of ideology. See his foundational essay "Ideology and Ideological State Apparatuses," in *Lenin and Philosophy and Other Essays*, trans. Ben Brewster (London: New Left Books, 1971). Foucault's notions like "technology of the self" (social mechanisms that shape our "subjectivities" to be happy within the objectives of power structures) and "episteme" (the grounds of knowledge and discourse that create the conditions for certain selfhoods to emerge), among many others, played a similar role within post-structuralist studies. A great introduction to these issues within the field of ideology is Chris Weedon, "Subjectivity and Identity," in *Identity and Culture: Narratives of Difference and Belonging* (New York: Open University Press, 2004), chap. 1. Within the field of political sociology, I have found political scientist Lilliana Mason's recent book *Uncivil Agreement*, chap. 2, to be a helpful summary of research on how social group identity and emotions are tied together to reinforce sorting or polarization.

10. That ideology forms within antagonism derives partly from the dialectical materialism of post-Hegel Marxism. Although I am not a Marxist/dialectical materialist, I believe social political life in autonomy from God runs on antagonism, and Marx and post-Marxists do much to illumine how these conditions work. Social reality, apart from Christ's presence, is inherently conflictual around a "lack," or in the words of Hegel, inherently split, always working for a resolution but only ever arriving at a temporary *aufhebung*. Ultimately, I suggest this political antagonism can only be resolved via the fullness of Christ, a political reality shaped in the real presence of Christ. For more on this, see my *End of Evangelicalism?*, 123–28. On the antagonistic nature of political reality, see Slavoj Žižek, *For They Know Not What They Do: Enjoyment as a Political Factor*, 2nd ed. (London: Verso Books, 1991), 31–36; Žižek, *Interrogating the Real*, ed. Rex Butler and Scott Stephens (New York: Continuum, 2006), 195.

11. For this concept I am relying on the idea of "performative contradiction" as found in writers like Denys Turner, *Marxism and Christianity* (Oxford: Oxford University Press, 1983), 26. Also, via a different angle, I'm drawing on the idea of "enlightened false consciousness," which seeks to reify an existing order, covering over injustices, by using excessive rationalizations to downplay contradictions. Political theorist Peter Sloterdijk offers an important insight in

this regard, however, in the spirit of ideological cynicism. He suggests that when the contradictions inevitably appear, people simply don't care. It's easier to ignore and believe what is most convenient for keeping the current life going. This insight has much to say in our current political times. See Peter Sloterdijk, *Critique of Cynical Reason* (Minneapolis: University of Minnesota Press, 1988), 5.

12. The entire example of the Caffeine Free Diet Coke is taken from Žižek, *Fragile Absolute*, 22–23. I am drawing on my previous observations made in *End of Evangelicalism?*, xxi–xxiii.

13. I am following an essential theme of my work in this paragraph: the idea that God's presence is the opposite of violence, striving, nonrelational enemy making. These things are evidence of the absence of Christ, for whom we must make space by surrender/submission to him as a group. See my *Faithful Presence*. When we give ourselves over to antagonism and strife as the way we lead our lives together, we in essence close off space from the presence of Christ working. Giving in to antagonism is giving in to a void, an emptiness in which chaos is allowed to reign. For an extensive biblical exposition of the way God's presence works in and through the Old Testament, how God's presence restrains chaos and violence, how his presence ultimately works in and through a people subject to him, see Gregory A. Boyd, *The Crucifixion of the Warrior God: Interpreting the Old Testament's Violent Portraits of God in Light of the Cross*, 2 vols. (Minneapolis: Fortress, 2017). Key to this understanding of the formation of a people is that, apart from God, our lives are in fact formed around a core that is empty and thereby ridden with chaos and driven by violence. Karl Barth labels the whole demonic realm of chaos and violence *das nichte* ("the nothing"). Barth, *Church Dogmatics* III/3, trans. G. W. Bromiley and R. J. Ehrlich, ed. G. W. Bromiley and T. F. Torrance (London: T&T Clark, 1960), 289–368. Boyd argues that the reality to which God says "no" (i.e., *das nichte*) cannot menace creation (cannot have any "real" material reality) unless created free agents give this "no" a reality by choosing to say "yes" to it. This in essence is what I have called "the empty politic" in *End of Evangelicalism?* See Gregory A. Boyd, *Satan and the Problem of Evil: Constructing a Trinitarian Warfare Theodicy* (Downers Grove, IL: InterVarsity, 2001), 287–90. Boyd details this in *Crucifixion of the Warrior God*, 2:1076n70. The opposite, therefore, of this politic that is formed around nothing by way of antagonisms is the politic of fullness, his presence (see the appendix). I outline the politic of fullness in detail in *End of Evangelicalism?* and summarize it on pp. 124–28. I describe the practice of this politic of fullness in *Faithful Presence*.

Chapter 3 Are You Biblical?

1. "This Is My Bible," Joel Osteen Ministries, accessed December 18, 2018, https://www.joelosteen.com/downloadables/Pages/Downloads/ThisIsMyBible_JOM.pdf.

2. Although the apostle Paul's authorship is often disputed in this text, no one doubts that the Pastoral Epistles originate within the Pauline school of authorship.

3. I acknowledge this list is a history of the Western church as led theologically by men (not women), many of them white men. This is the history of Western Christendom as inherited by the church of North America, whether white Protestantism or churches of color who live under the dominance of its influence. It is this Euro-white Western branch of Christianity that I see as primary in the breeding of the enemy-making machine.

4. Bill Cavanaugh disputes the modern understanding of the religious wars whereby religion is blamed as the source of violence and the liberal nation-state tames this violence and saves Western Christianity from its own violence. Instead, Cavanaugh sees the European princes as the ones seeking territory and wealth by violence and absorbing/subordinating the church to do its bidding. See William T. Cavanaugh, *Theopolitical Imagination: Discovering the Liturgy as a Political Act in an Age of Global Consumerism* (London: T&T Clark, 2003), 30–31. For a broader treatment see Cavanaugh, *The Myth of Religious Violence: Secular Ideology and the Roots of Modern Conflict* (Oxford: Oxford University Press, 2009). Ephraim Radner takes issue with Cavanaugh's separation of religion from its concomitant history of violence and argues instead for the church's complicity with it. The liberal society Cavanaugh complains about, Radner says, is a reality because the church has made it necessary. For more on this, see Ephraim Radner, *Brutal Unity: The Spiritual Politics of the Christian Church* (Waco: Baylor University Press, 2012), chaps. 1–3.

5. The history of the rise of this method of studying the Bible in post-Enlightenment Europe is outlined skillfully by Hans Frei in *The Eclipse of Biblical Narrative: A Study in Eighteenth and Nineteenth Century Hermeneutics* (New Haven: Yale University Press, 1980).

6. It is true, theologians such as John Calvin used the word "inerrancy" to describe the Bible before the late nineteenth century. But I would argue, along with several scholars, that it had never been aligned with modern historical-critical method before the articulation of Princeton theologians B. B. Warfield and A. A. Hodge.

7. Famously, Billy Graham had an intellectual crisis over the modernist historical-critical attack on the Bible as presented to him by his friend, former evangelist Charles Templeton. It is from this personal crisis that his famous phrase "The Bible says . . ." was born. For a fuller account of this episode, see my *The End of Evangelicalism? Discerning a New Faithfulness for Mission* (Eugene, OR: Cascade Books, 2011), 48–49.

8. The organization Compassion International, for example, puts it like this: "We believe in the Holy Scriptures *as originally given by God*, divinely inspired, infallible . . ." (emphasis added). "Our Statement of Faith," Compassion International, accessed November 20, 2018, https://www.compassion.com/statement -of-faith.htm.

9. See B. B. Warfield, "The Inerrancy of the Original Autographs," in *The Princeton Theology, 1812–1921*, ed. Mark Noll (Grand Rapids: Baker, 1983), 268–88. For the debates around the phrase "original autographs," see John Woodbridge, "Biblical Authority: Toward an Evaluation of the Rogers and McKim

Proposal," in *Biblical Authority and Conservative Perspectives: Viewpoints from the "Trinity Journal,"* ed. Douglas Moo (Grand Rapids: Kregel, 1997), 59–60.

10. Notice, for instance, the two most dominant evangelical groups working on the issue of women in ministry: The complementarian group, which does not support women in senior positions of leadership over men in the church, is called the Council on Biblical Manhood and Womanhood (CBMW). Its statement of faith contains the explicit verbiage that the Bible is "inerrant in the original writings." The egalitarian group, Christians for Biblical Equality (CBE), however, has moved away from this exact verbiage but has kept "authoritative for faith and practice." It is clear that the word "biblical" in both cases is now a substitute for "inerrant"—working in the same way to grant authority for its positions. Many of the founders and key figures of CBE were originally inerrantist and came from institutions that were as well, including Alvera Mickelsen (Wheaton College), Catherine Clark Kroeger (Gordon-Conwell), Gilbert Bilezikian (Wheaton College), Stan Gundry (Moody Bible Institute, Zondervan Publishing), and Roger Nicole (Gordon-Conwell).

11. Martin Copenhaver does a good job outlining Jesus's strategy of asking questions in *Jesus Is the Question: The 307 Questions Jesus Asked and the 3 He Answered* (Nashville: Abingdon, 2014).

12. Ironically, Henry Morris, founder of the creation science movement, chastised the Chicago Conference on Inerrancy (1978) when they refused to incorporate the "literal seven-day-creation" hypothesis into their statement on the Bible. He discusses this in *King of Creation* (San Diego: CLP, 1980). Even more ironic, Mark Noll reports that the founders of the inerrancy movement were evolutionists. See Noll, "Charles Hodge and B. B. Warfield on Science, the Bible, Evolution and Darwinism," *Modern Reformation* 7, no. 3 (1998): 18–22.

13. Bill Chappell, "Who 'Won' the Creation vs. Evolution Debate?," *The Two-Way*, February 6, 2014, http://www.npr.org/sections/thetwo-way/2014/02/06/272535141/who-won-the-creation-vs-evolution-debate.

14. Amy Ohlheiser, "The Creationists Have Already Won Tonight's Bill Nye vs. Ken Ham Debate," *The Atlantic*, February 4, 2014, https://www.theatlantic.com/national/archive/2014/02/creationists-have-already-won-tonights-bill-nye-vs-ken-ham-debate/357714/.

15. This is a quote used often by Michael Brown, PhD, in debates over whether gay sexuality can be Christian. Brown is director of the Coalition of Conscience and host of the nationally syndicated talk radio show *Line of Fire*. See, for instance, this debate on Moody Radio where he uses the phrase: https://www.youtube.com/watch?v=l-bTqIJP2JI.

16. An example of this is David Lose, "What Does the Bible Really Say about Homosexuality?," *HuffPost*, December 10, 2011, http://www.huffingtonpost.com/david-lose/what-does-the-bible-reall_b_990444.html.

17. A simple Google search reveals over thirty-eight thousand references to the "clobber passages" that are used in this way.

18. An example of these kinds of antagonisms that linger via the inerrancy view of the Bible is the book by Rachel Held Evans, *A Year of Biblical*

Womanhood: How a Liberated Woman Found Herself Sitting on Her Roof,
Covering Her Head, and Calling Her Husband Master (Nashville: Thomas
Nelson, 2012). The book chronicled her year of trying to read the Bible literally and follow various Old Testament commands given to women, including
menstruation laws—living in a separate tent so that no man will touch her—
sitting on a roof whenever she got contentious, calling her husband "master,"
and so forth. Although good-natured, the book plays on the antagonism of the
"inerrant Bible." She was playfully ridiculing the taking of every verse in the
Bible literally, a hermeneutic that finds its historical lineage in the "inerrancy"
world and her own fundamentalist background. Showing absurd contradictions
was pretty easy. And it caused antagonism and controversy (which helped sell
the book), evidenced by the fact that LifeWay banned the book from its bookstores. Meanwhile, it's questionable how many Christians (except in her own
Bible-Belt world) still actually believe in such a literal hermeneutic. And we
must ask whether the many people watching her interviews on CNN and other
media outlets were getting a prejudiced view of Christians culturally. Despite
her irenic nature, her good humor, and her appreciation of what she learned,
we must ask whether the witness of Christianity suffered from this caricature
she was attacking. This, I contend, is the way the enemy-making machine works
within the ideology machine.

19. This is a paraphrase (in the quotes) of an aspect of Christopher Hitchens'
argument in *God Is Not Great* (New York: Hachette, 2009), 102.

Chapter 4 God's Grand Drama: The Bible as the Space beyond Enemies

1. A whole slew of theologians, post-1960s, began pushing against the En-
lightenment heritage view of the Bible as a piece of historical literature subject
to the standards of historical-critical science. See, for instance, Hans Frei, *The*
Eclipse of Biblical Narrative: A Study in Eighteenth and Nineteenth Century
Hermeneutics (New Haven: Yale University Press, 1980); Hans Urs von Balthasar,
The Glory of the Lord: A Theological Aesthetics, ed. Joseph Fessio SJ and John
Riches, vol. 1, *Seeing the Form*, trans. Erasmo Leiva-Merikakis (San Francisco:
Ignatius, 1998); Christopher J. H. Wright, *The Mission of God: Unlocking the*
Bible's Grand Narrative (Downers Grove, IL: IVP Academic, 2006); and Kevin
Vanhoozer, *Drama of Doctrine: A Canonical-Linguistic Approach to Christian*
Theology (Louisville: Westminster John Knox, 2005), which are all pushing this
agenda to see the Bible as Grand Drama, as the Story that we have been invited
into. This diminishes neither the historicity of the text nor its authority within
the church. Instead, it relativizes the authority of external sources upon the text
(such as historical-critical methodology) and enhances the historical authority
of the text as carried within the church. And it makes a place for the experience
of that authority among Christians within the practice of preaching/reading
Scripture within the church.

2. This account is influenced by Michael Gorman's compelling commentary on the book of Revelation, *Reading Revelation Responsibly* (Eugene, OR:

Cascade Books, 2011). In it he describes how there is no final battle of Armageddon in the book of Revelation (142). Rather, it is by the sword that comes from Christ's (the Lamb's) mouth, through the persuasion of the Word, that victory shall come (155). Gorman describes how Jesus is present as one walking in and among his churches, symbolized via the lampstands (83). Jesus as Lamb rules patiently until all have been given time to repent and come in.

3. The "word of God is living and active, sharper than any two-edged sword" (Heb. 4:12 NRSV). The sword, though it divides, is not violent. It does not kill or make enemies via coercion. It divides truth from untruth. Michael Gorman shows this to be true in the book of Revelation. Gorman points out that the sword of the Word in Revelation 19:11–16, 21, comes from the mouth of Jesus. It is a sword of persuasion not violence. And because Jesus, the rider, is still "clothed in a robe dipped in blood" (v. 13 NRSV), he bears the marks of suffering that is of spoken and lived witness, God's way of working in the world. The sword therefore "signifies the effective word of God's judgment . . . that needs no literal sword, and which a literal sword could never accomplish." The battles of Revelation signify the reality of God's defeat of evil, but actual physical war is not the means of that defeat. Indeed, the battle of Armageddon never comes. Gorman therefore suggests that Christ's "only weapon is the 'sword' of his word." Gorman, *Reading Revelation Responsibly*, 153–55.

4. Vanhoozer, *Drama of Doctrine*, 1–75.

5. Vanhoozer, *Drama of Doctrine*, 362.

6. I have learned this idea most succinctly through the work of Christopher J. H. Wright. See especially his *Mission of God*.

7. Notice, for instance, the difference between Kevin Vanhoozer and Scot McKnight in the architecture of the Story. McKnight challenges the classic Reformed organization of the Story, à la Vanhoozer, that reads Creation, Fall, Redemption, and Consummation (CFRC) as the primary parts of the narrative. McKnight argues that CFRC is actually a side story to what he labels the ABA story, which goes like this: Plan A was Adam, Abraham, and Samuel, through whom God reveals himself reigning as king. But Israel wants a king, so God makes a concession in 1 Sam. 8 and offers a king; this is Plan B. The Israelite kings fail, and so Plan A is revised and the kingship takes on the form of the coming of the Son as messiah. See McKnight, *Kingdom Conspiracy: Returning to the Radical Mission of the Local Church* (Grand Rapids: Brazos, 2016), 32–38. For McKnight, the dominant theme of God's reigning and bringing his rule over the world is the dominant Story/Grand Drama rather than the redemption of a sin-corrupted creation (i.e., CFRC), which is only part of the story. These two respective emphases in church history reflect the theology/histories of the Reformed versus Anabaptist churches. Elsewhere McKnight renames the three parts of the story Theocracy, Monarchy, and Christocracy. See *The Blue Parakeet: Rethinking How You Read the Bible*, 2nd ed. (Grand Rapids: Zondervan, 2018), 69, 70. The irony is that, at the time of this writing, McKnight and Vanhoozer are part of the same church.

8. The best exposition of this way of reading the Old Testament, especially in regard to accounts of genocide and horrific holy wars, is Gregory A. Boyd,

The Crucifixion of the Warrior God: Interpreting the Old Testament's Violent Portraits of God in Light of the Cross (Minneapolis: Fortress, 2017), vol. 1, part 2.

9. Karl Barth, *Church Dogmatics* I/1, 2nd ed., trans. G. W. Bromiley, ed. G. W. Bromiley and T. F. Torrance (London: T&T Clark, 1975), 120.

10. Barth, *Church Dogmatics* I/1, 107–8.

11. Willie James Jennings and J. Kameron Carter show how, in the history of Christianity, it was the idea that the church replaced Israel as the means by which God would bring salvation to the world that made possible a melding of racism with Euro-white Christianity. Jennings argues that when the Christian's identity and history in Israel are forgotten, Christianity becomes abstracted into an ahistorical "belief system"—in other words, an ideology. This phenomenon, known as supersessionism, becomes "the womb in which whiteness will mature." Willie James Jennings, *The Christian Imagination: Theology and the Origins of Race* (New Haven: Yale University Press, 2010), 36. Strangely, via the Reformation, the gospel morphed into a concept (forensic atonement) that was cast over against Judaism (and "the law"). Separated then from Israel, Christians could now locate their identity differently, no longer as a people grafted into Israel but now as a people fully within European white identity. Europe was now the place God had chosen to reveal himself. According to Jennings, "Here was a process of discerning Christian identity that, because it had jettisoned Israel from its calculus of the formation of Christian life, created a conceptual vacuum that was filled by the European" (*Christian Imagination*, 33). In Carter's words, "[The West's] accomplishment [supersessionism] was one in which . . . Christians no longer had to interpret their existence within another story—Israel's. Rather, its accomplishment was to make Israel's story a moment within understanding the story of Western civilization as the story of white accomplishment." J. Kameron Carter, *Race: A Theological Account* (Cambridge: Oxford University Press, 2008), 261. A big and necessary component to what I am arguing here is that if the Bible is to be God's Grand Drama that opens space beyond enemies, it must maintain the integrity of the entire Bible, Hebrew and Greek testaments together. It must maintain the integrity of the whole Story. Here the original vision of the church can be sustained, as a people of all tribes and nations grafted onto the one people of God, an extension of Israel, an absorbing of all people into one unified people of God (Gal. 3:26). In each diaspora town and village we are able not to coerce a people to become us on our terms but instead to enter as exiles, seeking the welfare of the city on its own terms, by which its people become a new expression of the nations of God in Israel as fulfilled in Christ.

12. Christ, for Balthasar, is "the center of all revelation" in whom, by whom, and with whom we see the world as it is. It is not surprising then that the title of one of Balthasar's key headings in *The Glory of the Lord* is "Christ the Center of the Form of Revelation" (1:541).

13. In Balthasar's own words, "Scripture does not stand over against this form of revelation [the pure form of Christ] by way of imitation as a second

autonomous form, complete in itself: for Scripture itself belongs to the sphere of revelation and, being the normative testimony, it is part of that revelation." Balthasar, *The Glory of the Lord*, 1:541. The words in brackets are mine for purposes of clarification.

14. I have discussed what this kind of preaching is and its importance for a church in mission in *The Great Giveaway: Reclaiming the Mission of the Church from Big Business, Parachurch Organizations, Consumer Capitalism, and Other Modern Maladies* (Grand Rapids: Baker Books, 2005), chap. 5, and in *Faithful Presence: Seven Disciplines That Shape the Church for Mission* (Downers Grove, IL: InterVarsity, 2016), chap. 5. In addition, I have written numerous posts online describing methods and ways of preaching in this vein.

Chapter 5 Have You Made a Decision?

1. "Kathie Lee Gifford: How Billy Graham Led Me to Christ," Kathie Lee Gifford, as told to Kate Shellnutt, *Christianity Today*, February 19, 2016, http:// www.christianitytoday.com/ct/2016/march/kathie-lee-gifford-how-billy-graham -led-me-to-christ.html.

2. Ron Sider famously outlines multiple statistics of the failure of evangelicals to live any differently than the rest of the population in the United States in *The Scandal of the Evangelical Conscience: Why Are Christians Living Just Like the Rest of the World?* (Grand Rapids: Baker Books, 2005), 11–17. A brief outline of his case, excerpted from the book, can be found at *Books & Culture* 11, no. 1 (January/February 2005), https://www.booksandculture.com/articles/2005 /janfeb/3.8.html.

3. The history of the altar call in North America is detailed by R. Allan Streett, *The Effective Invitation: A Practical Guide for the Pastor* (Grand Rapids: Kregel, 1984), chap. 2, and David Bennett, *The Altar Call: Its Origins and Present Usage* (Camp Hill, PA: Camp Hill Publications, 2000). They disagree over some details of the history.

4. The Scottish missiologist Andrew Walls describes conversion as peculiar to nineteenth- and twentieth-century American revivalism. "Conversion," he asserts, "referred to an experience that basically moved a person from nominal Christianity professed generally throughout society . . . thru a deep consciousness of one's personal sin . . . to a joyous realization/acceptance of God's forgiveness in Christ." Walls describes how Western evangelicals normalized this pattern of experience and then, sending missionaries to other parts of the world, expected to see this same pattern lived out even in places where there was no nominal Christianity prior to such a conversion. Andrew Walls, "Converts or Proselytes? The Crisis over Conversion in the Early Church," *Missiology* 28, no. 1 (2004): 2.

5. Most notably, the famous Protestant preacher Harry Emerson Fosdick claimed that the notion of penal substitution—that shed blood "placates an alienated deity"—was a crude anthropomorphism that turns God into an avenging tyrant. Gary J. Dorrien, *The Remaking of Evangelical Theology* (Louisville:

Westminster John Knox, 1998), 38. In return, J. Gresham Machen, a well-known apologist for fundamentalist evangelicalism, argued, "According to Christian belief, Jesus is our Savior, not by virtue of what He said, or even by virtue of what He was, but by what He did. He is our Savior, not because He inspired us to live the kind of life He lived, but because He took upon Himself the dreadful guilt of our sins and bore it instead of us on the cross. Such is the Christian conception of the cross of Christ. It is ridiculed as being a 'subtle theory of the atonement.' In reality, it is the plain teaching of the word of God; we know absolutely nothing about an atonement that is not a vicarious atonement, for that is the only atonement of which the New Testament speaks." J. Gresham Machen, *Christianity and Liberalism* (1923; repr., Grand Rapids: Eerdmans, 2001), 117. For more on this controversy in the 1920s, see Dorrien, *Remaking of Evangelical Theology*, 38–39.

6. The Catholic Church's catechism describes an indulgence as "a remission before God of the temporal punishment due to sins whose guilt has already been forgiven, which the faithful Christian who is duly disposed gains under certain prescribed conditions through the action of the Church which, as the minister of redemption, dispenses and applies with authority the treasury of the satisfactions of Christ and the saints." *Catechism of the Catholic Church* (New York: Doubleday, 2003), 411–13. Indulgences were granted in return for good works and prayers, thereby reducing the penance required by the church to complete one's reconciliation. In Luther's time, they were excessively abused by the church, purchased as a way of lowering the amount of time spent in purgatory upon death. The church used them to raise money for the building of St. Peter's in Rome and other sundry projects in the fifteenth and sixteenth centuries.

7. In my *The End of Evangelicalism? Discerning a New Faithfulness for Mission* (Eugene, OR: Cascade Books, 2011), 85, I trace how justification was split from sanctification in the *ordo salutis* (Latin for "order of salvation") of the Reformation. This, I suggest, created the potential later in the history of Protestantism for duplicity in the Christian life. One could interpret the holiness and revivalist movements as a response to this problem, with the emphasis on a second work of grace (and a second decision or surrender of one's life).

8. Samuel Smith, "James Dobson Says Paula White Led Donald Trump to Jesus Christ," *Christian Post*, June 29, 2016, https://www.christianpost.com/news/james-dobson-says-paula-white-led-donald-trump-to-jesus-christ-165844/.

9. David Frost and Fred Bauer, *Billy Graham: Personal Thoughts of a Private Man* (Colorado Springs: Chariot Victor Publishing, 1997), 72.

10. As reported in Ray Comfort, *Hell's Best Kept Secret* (New Kensington, PA: Whitaker House, 1989), 9.

11. "Ted Haggard's Sex Scandal," *Larry King Live*, interview transcript, January 29, 2009, http://transcripts.cnn.com/TRANSCRIPTS/0901/29/lkl.01.html.

12. The day after his affirmation, however, Eugene Peterson retracted it. See Kate Shellnutt, "Actually, Eugene Peterson Does Not Support Same-Sex Marriage," *Christianity Today*, July 13, 2017, https://www.christianitytoday.com/news/2017/july/eugene-peterson-actually-does-not-support-gay-marriage.html.

Chapter 6 Participating in His Reign: Conversion as the Space beyond Enemies

1. I follow here the outline of the gospel offered by Scot McKnight in *The King Jesus Gospel: The Original Good News Revisited* (Grand Rapids: Zondervan, 2012), chap. 4, but I also draw on the work of other New Testament scholars who have helped shape the new perspective on Paul, such as N. T. Wright.

2. Besides Scot McKnight and N. T. Wright, I recommend reading Matthew Bates, who outlines this gospel in similar form via the New Testament in *Salvation by Allegiance Alone: Rethinking Faith, Works, and the Gospel of Jesus the King* (Grand Rapids: Baker Academic, 2017), chap. 2.

3. McKnight argues in his *King Jesus Gospel* for this being the definitive outline of the gospel for the apostles and the early church. In so doing he is following C. H. Dodd, *The Apostolic Preaching and Its Developments* (London: Hodder & Stoughton, 1936).

4. On this, see McKnight, *King Jesus Gospel*, chap. 9.

5. See Bates, *Salvation by Allegiance Alone*, chap. 3, for a wonderfully detailed summary of how the resurrection/ascension/exaltation of Christ is the fulcrum of the gospels proclaimed in the New Testament.

6. For a deeper understanding of the role forgiveness plays in the gospel, and specifically the role of Christ as substitutionary/representative sacrifice for our sins, see N. T. Wright, *The Day the Revolution Began: Reconsidering the Meaning of Jesus's Crucifixion* (New York: HarperOne, 2016), 314–40. Wright teases out how the sacrifice of Jesus on the cross is as a covering; God has "passed over the sins previously committed" (Rom. 3:25 NRSV). He is the means of purification for a nation, the means by which this people can enter his presence (playing the role of the mercy seat/*hilasterion* sacrifice before entry into the temple). This places Jesus's sacrifice not as the appeasement of God's wrath or as the substitution to take on a punishment for another but as the means by which we are restored to his presence. Forgiveness is the means to be restored to his presence.

7. James H. Cone, *The Cross and the Lynching Tree* (New York: Orbis, 2011), 154. Anthony Bradley, in a stroke of genius, published a thread on "the consequences of today's truncated gospel" in which he details the history of the truncated gospel's complicity with the history of racism and the evangelical-fundamentalist church. He did this in the form of a black church "sermon close." He offered a lengthy bibliography on the issue. The entire thread is available at https://threadreaderapp.com/thread/1035622717293297673.html (accessed September 1, 2018). For a sociological examination of the impact of evangelical belief on engagement with racism, see Michael O. Emerson and Christian Smith, *Divided by Faith: Evangelical Religion and the Problem of Race in America* (Oxford: Oxford University Press, 2001). For another take on the problematic relationship between substitionary atonement and injustice in the world, see Rita Nakashima Brock and Rebecca Ann Parker, *Proverbs of Ashes: Violence, Redemptive Suffering, and the Search for What Saves Us* (Boston: Beacon, 2001).

8. Cone, *Cross and the Lynching Tree*, 155.

9. Ruth Padilla DeBorst, "Living Creation-Community in God's World Today," *Journal of Latin American Theology* 5, no. 1 (2010): 60.

10. "It is not simply that evangelism and social involvement are to be done alongside each other. Rather, in integral mission our proclamation has social consequences as we call people to love and repentance in all areas of life." "Micah Network Declaration on Integral Mission," September 27, 2001, http://www .micahnetwork.org/sites/default/files/doc/page/mn_integral_mission_declara tion_en.pdf.

11. Again, Bates, *Salvation by Allegiance Alone,* shows how the meaning of "faith" for the Christian in the West has been distorted by the Western emphasis on "forgiveness of sins" as the outworking of the gospel rather than on one's giving faith, trust, obedience, and "allegiance" to the One who has been made Lord of the universe, which opens up this space for God to rule and work among us for his kingdom.

12. It is, of course, such a powerful depiction in John 12:32 that Jesus sees—in and through his being lifted up on the cross, receiving nonviolently all the consequences and violence of the world's sin—that people will be drawn to him and his presence.

13. In stressing "the faithfulness of the Son of God" I am alluding to the already well-worn work of Richard B. Hays, *The Faith of Jesus Christ: The Narrative Substructure of Galatians 3:1–4:11*, 2nd ed. (Grand Rapids: Eerdmans, 2002). On this text see Hays, "The Letter to the Galatians: Introduction, Commentary and Reflections," in *The New Interpreter's Bible*, vol. 11, *Second Corinthians–Philemon* (Nashville: Abingdon, 2000), 244.

14. This way of talking about salvation draws heavily on the work of Michael Gorman, who proposes that "justification by faith" must be understood, within the apostle Paul's writings, in terms of participating in co-crucifixion with Christ. Salvation is akin to *theosis*, being saved "in Christ" in and through his cruciformity. And yet, cruciformity is more than personal; it is indeed the very character of God and the way he works in the world via his presence. It is therefore by participating in his cruciform presence in the world that we are changed and that the world is drawn into his work. See Michael Gorman, *Inhabiting the Cruciform God: Kenosis, Justification, and Theosis in Paul's Narrative Soteriology* (Grand Rapids: Eerdmans, 2009), 45–55, 161–70. See also his wonderful book *Becoming the Gospel: Paul, Participation, and Mission* (Grand Rapids: Eerdmans, 2015).

15. Because God works only through his presence, he will not coerce people into life with him. He has chosen to make himself visible through a people who in return invite others to recognize his work, submit to him as Lord, and be forgiven by and reconciled to him in all things. This is the way God has chosen to change the world. For my own biblical exposition of this, see *Faithful Presence: Seven Disciplines That Shape the Church for Mission* (Downers Grove, IL: InterVarsity, 2016). For a deep biblical exposition of the way God works in the world, see Gregory A. Boyd, *The Crucifixion of the Warrior God: Interpreting*

the Old Testament's Violent Portraits of God in Light of the Cross, 2 vols. (Minneapolis: Fortress, 2017).

16. A helpful way of understanding these dynamics is through Paul Hiebert's concept of bounded-set and centered-set understandings of social space. As I explain in the appendix, the bounded-set experience sets boundaries in the world between those who have assented to a belief and those who have not. In the terms of evangelical Christianity, the decision has served as that boundary that defines what it means to be a part of the in-group. In the centered-set experience, however, being a Christian is defined by the direction of one's movement toward Jesus—the center—through the knowledge and love of God. There is a difference between those who are moving toward this center and those who are not, but it is a permeable difference. The boundary is there, but the focus lies on the center and not on defining and protecting the boundaries. With the centered-set view, there is a recognition of the fact that different people are at different points of the journey. This becomes a helpful way to further understand how God is working in the world and aligns well with the theology of salvation I am working with here. Hiebert first expounded his position in Paul G. Hiebert, *Anthropological Reflections on Missiological Issues* (Grand Rapids: Baker Academic, 1996), chap. 6. For further discussion, see the appendix.

17. I describe the practice of proclaiming the gospel and its dependence on God's presence in *Faithful Presence*, chap. 5.

18. I go into detail about this practice and its relation to Christ's eucharistic presence in *Faithful Presence*, chap. 3. Also, central to discipleship is the regular practice of reconciliation in his presence among a body of people, which I describe in *Faithful Presence*, chap. 4.

19. Daniel T. Niles, *That They May Have Life* (New York: Harper & Row, 1951), quoted in David Black, "The Callings," *New York Times*, May 11, 1986, https://www.nytimes.com/1986/05/11/magazine/the-callings.html.

Chapter 7 Let's Make America Christian Again?

1. See Yale historian Joseph Yannielli's "Princeton and Abolition," written for Princeton University's *Princeton & Slavery* project, accessed March 24, 2018, https://slavery.princeton.edu/stories/princeton-and-abolition.

2. Donald Dayton substantiates this history in *Discovering an Evangelical Heritage* (New York: Harper & Row, 1976). See also David Moberg, *The Great Reversal* (Philadelphia: Lippincott, 1972), 28–30; George Marsden, *Fundamentalism and American Culture* (New York: Oxford University Press, 1980), 85–93, 124–32.

3. The classic text on this is Ernest Lee Tuyeson, *Redeemer Nation: The Idea of America's Millennial Role* (Chicago: University of Chicago Press, 1968). See also Dayton, *Discovering*, 124.

4. Most notably, Moberg, *Great Reversal*. See also on this topic Dayton, *Discovering*, chap. 10; Marsden, *Fundamentalism*, chaps. 9–11.

5. Carl F. H. Henry, *The Uneasy Conscience of Modern Fundamentalism* (Grand Rapids: Eerdmans, 1947).

6. Francis Schaeffer, Os Guinness, Harold Ockenga, and Carl F. H. Henry were just some of the leaders emerging post–World War II to lead evangelicals in this direction.

7. Jerry Falwell, *Listen, America!* (New York: Doubleday, 1980), 243–44.

8. The source for this widely cited quote is Benjamin R. Barber, *Jihad vs. McWorld* (New York: Times, 1995), 212.

9. Dayton, *Discovering*, 124.

10. Rev. Hill famously said these words on the TBN television network: "Pastor E.V. Hill: After 9/11/2001," YouTube video, 0:9:58, posted by pastor-hillclassics, April 25, 2010, https://www.youtube.com/watch?v=hA-2l61oig4; quote at 0:7:27.

11. I tell this story in David Fitch and Geoff Holsclaw, *Prodigal Christianity: 10 Signposts into the Missional Frontier* (San Francisco: Jossey-Bass, 2013), 144.

12. The statistical data on this amazing fact is outlined in John Fea, *Believe Me: The Evangelical Road to Donald Trump* (Grand Rapids: Eerdmans, 2018), 133–64.

13. Though much disputed, the most often quoted statistic about the election was that 81 percent of evangelicals voted for Donald Trump as president.

14. This is central to the way ideology works in making the subject think his/her allegiances were in fact his/her own choice all along. But in reality, the subject owes its existence, its feelings, and its sense of location to the ideological apparatus that gives the ideology its power to hold the subject in its grasp. Marx, Lacan, Althusser, and others illumine how this works. On this see Slavoj Žižek, *The Sublime Object of Ideology* (London: Verso Books, 1989), chaps. 3, 5.

15. The Religious Freedom Restoration Act

16. As quoted in Stephanie Ebbs, "Indiana Gov. Mike Pence Says Controversial 'Religious Freedom' Law Won't Change," ABC News, March 29, 2015, https://abcnews.go.com/Politics/indiana-gov-mike-pence-controversial-religious-freedom-law/story?id=29985752.

17. This descriptor is very important to me because the eye of a hurricane is hollow, empty. There's nothing there. It nonetheless holds the storm together.

18. Just to be clear, I acknowledge that not all churches of the time were working for justice in this way. I speak specifically about the powerful movements that emerged among the holiness movements of the seventeenth and eighteenth centuries as discussed in this chapter, specifically in n. 2.

Chapter 8 The Local Church Is My Politics: Church as the Space beyond Enemies

1. Romans 13:1 is not a challenge to this notion but an instruction as to the church's posture toward government. "Let every person be subject to the governing authorities" (NRSV) is written to a church under Roman rule, which was at the time persecuting some Christians. The apostle Paul is therefore saying, In all things, submit, even to death, especially when you must disobey the government when it acts against God. Romans 13 is to be read as directly flowing from

Rom. 12. For a good summary of this position, see John Howard Yoder, *The Politics of Jesus* (Grand Rapids: Eerdmans, 2003), chap. 10.

2. For the meaning of the Greek word *ekklesia* in both Greco-Roman and Jewish contexts current with the Pauline Epistles, see *The Oxford Illustrated History of Greece and the Hellenistic World* (Cambridge: Oxford University Press, 2001), 130–36; L. Coenen, "Church," in *New International Dictionary of New Testament Theology*, ed. Colin Brown (Grand Rapids: Zondervan, 1986), 1:291. For an expansive treatment of the subject, see Young-Ho Park, *Paul's Ekklesia as a Civic Assembly* (Tubingen: Mohr Siebeck, 2014).

3. In the words of Anabaptist theologian John Howard Yoder, the church "has ways of making decisions, defining membership, and carrying out common tasks." *Body Politics: Five Practices of the Christian Community before the Watching World* (Scottdale, PA: Herald Press, 1992), viii. I quote Yoder with discernment, recognizing his personal history of abuse toward women within his orbit of influence while a professor at Mennonite Seminary in Elkhart, Indiana, and at the University of Notre Dame. For a treatment of the problem of quoting Yoder that I am sympathetic with, please read Lisa Shirach, "Afterword: To the Next Generation of Pacifist Theologians," in *John Howard Yoder: Radical Theologian*, ed. J. Denny Weaver (Eugene, OR: Cascade Books, 2014), 377–95.

4. Augustine, *City of God*, trans. Henry Betteman (London: Penguin, 2004), 19.19, p. 878.

5. Most of the details of Clarence Jordan's life in the following paragraphs have been drawn from Charles Marsh, *The Beloved Community: How Faith Shapes Social Justice, from the Civil Rights Movement to Today* (New York: Basic Books, 2005), chap. 2.

6. Quoted in Marsh, *Beloved Community*, 66.

7. Marsh, *Beloved Community*, 174.

8. Over the years, as these three words—relocation, redistribution, reconciliation—have changed in their nuance, CCDA has developed and reshaped them and has added eight components to the training. See https://ccda.org/.

9. Marsh, *Beloved Community*, 176.

10. I have differentiated the Anabaptist "first/then" from the Reformed "both/and" in my article "'Knitting While Detroit Burns?': The Reformed 'Both/And' versus the Anabaptist 'First/Then,'" Missio Alliance, August 27, 2013, https://www.missioalliance.org/knitting-while-detroit-burns-the-reformed-%E2%80%9Cbothand%E2%80%80%9D-versus-the-anabaptist-%E2%80%80%9Cfirst-then%E2%80%80%9D/.

11. Quoted in Marsh, *Beloved Community*, 67.

12. Oscar Cullmann, *Christ and Time: The Primitive Christian Conception of Time and History* (London: SCM, 1951), 39–49.

13. My views on this eschatological way of understanding the church/world distinction are heavily influenced by John Howard Yoder's essay "Peace without Eschatology," which can be found as "If Christ Is Truly Lord," chap. 3 in John Howard Yoder, *The Original Revolution* (Scottdale, PA: Herald Press, 2003).

14. "First fruits" is a metaphor Paul continually uses to describe the church as first in order of a whole harvest to come in the future. Whether it is in being saved first, ahead of the rest (2 Thess. 2:13), or in the receiving of the Spirit ahead of the world (Rom. 8:23), or in Christ's resurrection ahead of those who shall come later (1 Cor. 15:20), in every occasion Paul uses "first fruits" to speak of the chronological order of the church's participation now proleptically in things that will come to fruition in the future.

15. Barth talked about this dynamic using the classic patristic terms *anhypostasia* and *enhypostasia*. *Anhypostasia* emphasizes that the human nature of Jesus Christ has no independent existence apart from the preexistent Word in the incarnation. See, for example, *Church Dogmatics* IV/2, trans. G. W. Bromiley, ed. G. W. Bromiley and T. F. Torrance (London: T&T Clark, 1958), 49–50. This use of *anhypostasia* safeguards the utter dependence of the creature upon the Creator. Barth characterized the church/Jesus relation in the same terms. The relationship, therefore, between Christ and the church always carries an asymmetrical character. The church is always totally dependent on Christ for its existence, and yet Christ is never in any way dependent on the church for his existence. See, for example, *Church Dogmatics* IV/2, 59–60.

16. We know that at times in the Old and New Testaments, God withdraws his presence from the one who perseveres relentlessly in his or her own rebellion and sin, thus "giving over" that person to their sin. Yet even this is done as the means to draw that person back to himself. See Greg Boyd's extensive treatment of this subject in *The Crucifixion of the Warrior God: Interpreting the Old Testament's Violent Portraits of God in Light of the Cross*, 2 vols. (Minneapolis: Fortress, 2017), part 5.

17. See above, chap. 4, n. 2.

18. This episode is recorded in many places, including "Clarence Jordan: Community Founder and Racial Justice Advocate," *Plough*, accessed June 12, 2018, https://www.plough.com/en/topics/faith/witness/clarence-jordan.

19. I have described this practice in detail, and how this is about Christ's presence and the kingdom, in *Faithful Presence: Seven Disciplines That Shape the Church for Mission* (Downers Grove, IL: InterVarsity, 2016), chap. 4.

20. The words "binding and loosing" are rabbinic terms for discernment of multiple kinds of conflicts and disagreements in the community. See Yoder, *Body Politics*, chap. 2.

21. For my work, this is the primary means of diagnosis for a faithful political theology in the post-Christendom West. We must diagnose whether we are in fact leading our churches into a politic of fullness or into an empty politic. For me this is the central issue facing the church in terms of political theology today. For further explanation and exposition on what this might mean, see my *The End of Evangelicalism? Discerning a New Faithfulness for Mission* (Eugene, OR: Cascade Books, 2011), 40–47, 124–28.

22. Markus Barth, *Ephesians: Introduction, Translation, and Commentary on Chapters 1–3* (New York: Doubleday, 1985), 204.

23. Markus Barth makes this case (while also referring to other scholars) in *Ephesians*, 203–5.

24. Most prominently in A. W. Tozer's famous *The Pursuit of God* (Harrisburg, PA: Christian Publications, 1948), 49–53 and elsewhere.

25. I have written extensively on this practice of church in *Faithful Presence*.

26. In this way there is no real "fencing of the table." Rather, it is the power of his presence that makes necessary the discerning of our relationship with Jesus and with one another before we present ourselves to his presence. As said earlier, enemies might be revealed at the table, but they are not made. This is the nature of the table and why some get sick and die when they come not discerning the table (1 Cor. 11:29–30).

27. The *epiclesis* is the historic prayer in Roman and Eastern liturgies invoking the Spirit to become present, making the bread and cup the real body and blood of Christ. There are, of course, different versions of the prayer within various traditions, accompanied by different meanings as to the effect of the prayer of *epiclesis* around the table.

Chapter 9 Beyond the Church of Us vs. Them

1. This classic study was republished as Muzafer Sherif, O. J. Harvey, B. Jack White, William R. Hood, and Carolyn W. Sherif, *The Robbers Cave Experiment: Intergroup Conflict and Cooperation* (Middleton, CT: Wesley University Press, 1988).

2. I refer to the tragedy that came to light in 2018 among leaders at Willow Creek Community Church and the revelation of the problems of leadership as promoted and taught by the Willow Creek Global Leadership Summit. I assume we are all now looking more carefully at how we mimic business CEO–style leadership in North America.

3. Though the text is viewed as apocryphal by most (that is, not part of the original Johannine Gospel), a significant number nonetheless accept it as authentic to the historical Jesus. See Chris Keith, "Recent and Previous Research on the *Pericope Adulterae* (John 7.53–8.11)," *Currents in Biblical Research* 6, no. 3 (2008): 394. This one simple text illustrates so many of the lessons of Jesus's leadership, and I believe that everything I say about Jesus in this text can be substantiated elsewhere in the Gospels. I hope to explore this in a future book.

4. I am following Michel de Certeau's distinction between "strategies" and "tactics." Strategies are the ways people in power operate, their plans for how they want things to work, the measurable results they expect, and so forth. Tactics are the tools of the weak. Because they cannot control the future, they seek to disrupt the reigning system one piece at a time. Michel de Certeau, *The Practice of Everyday Life* (Berkeley: University of California Press, 1988), 35–37.

Appendix 1 The Fullness of Him Who Fills All in All: Rudiments of a Political Theology of Presence

1. As noted above (chap. 8, n. 23), Markus Barth makes this case in *Ephesians: Introduction, Translation, and Commentary on Chapters 1–3* (New York: Doubleday, 1985), 203–5.

2. I describe the "politic of fullness" versus the "empty politic" throughout *The End of Evangelicalism? Discerning a New Faithfulness for Mission* (Eugene, OR: Cascade Books, 2011). There is a brief summary on pp. 124–28 of this book. This whole politic of fullness in the world is dependent upon a particular construal of the Trinity that I have described elsewhere as "the twofold movement of the Son into the world." To read more on my development of the doctrine of the Trinity in this regard, see David Fitch, *Faithful Presence: Seven Disciplines That Shape the Church for Mission* (Downers Grove, IL: IVP Books, 2016), 197–206; David Fitch, "The Other Missional Conversation: Making Way for the Neo-Anabaptist Contribution to the Missional Movement in North America," *Missiology* 44, no. 4 (January 1, 2016): 466–78.

3. I have outlined these practices, in the historical line of the sacraments, in *Faithful Presence*.

4. It is important to recognize in my work that "antagonism" is different from "conflict" or "disagreement." Disagreement and conflict are a normal part of being finite social beings in dependence on one another in sorting out the contingencies of life and meaning. Under the lordship of Christ, in his presence, God is in such conflict, often using it to work his purposes in his people. When sin enters in, antagonism results. These disagreements or conflicts become antagonism when they turn into oppositional enemy making. Violence, hate, and coercion are at the center of this sociality of antagonism. This is not of God.

5. Some might argue that Paul's challenge in 2 Cor. 6:17 to "come out from them and be separate," following his declaration to Corinth that they are the temple of the living God, suggests this very thing. But Paul has actually just finished calling them into the life of God's work of reconciliation in the world (the end of 2 Cor. 5:11–21). Thus, Paul is actually calling them out of the antagonism-driven life, the life of darkness (emptiness), the life of lawlessness (autonomy and narcissism), with his statement "Come out from them and be separate."

6. These thoughts and quotes come from Harvard Jewish studies scholar Jon D. Levenson in "The Temple and the World," *The Journal of Religion* 64, no. 3 (July 1984): 275–98. He expounds further on them in *Sinai and Zion: An Entry into the Jewish Bible* (New York: HarperOne, 1987). My thanks to Geoff Holsclaw for putting me onto these insights.

7. Beale's thesis was first carried out in a paper delivered at the 2004 Evangelical Theological Society meetings and then published as G. K. Beale, "Eden, the Temple, and the Church's Mission in the New Creation," *Journal of the Evangelical Theological Society* 48, no. 1 (March 2005): 5–31. I don't necessarily agree with the individualist account of how God's presence is to be extended in this article, but the general idea of the article has been foundational to my understanding of church and presence. For a fuller explication, see G. K. Beale, *The Temple and the Church's Mission: A Biblical Theology of the Dwelling Place* (Downers Grove, IL: IVP Academic, 2004).

8. See Barth, *Ephesians*, 203–5.

9. Paul Hiebert, "Conversion, Culture and Cognitive Categories," *Gospel in Context* 11, no. 4 (October 1978): 24–29, offers a succinct presentation of the concept of bounded set and centered set.

10. It is impossible in the space available here to deal with the problem of violence in the Old Testament appearing to be at the hands of God. Obviously, this would seem to contradict the notion that God works nonviolently through his presence in the world. For the best exposition of this problem, and indeed how God works through the "withdrawal" of his presence ("redemptive withdrawal"), see Gregory A. Boyd, *The Crucifixion of the Warrior God: Interpreting the Old Testament's Violent Portraits of God in Light of the Cross*, 2 vols. (Minneapolis: Fortress, 2017), part 5.

index